Rev. Oscar Amisi

leadership role! It is full of practical information for those engaged in active leadership roles or for those starting the journey. I can honestly say my only regret is not having read this at the beginning of my leadership journey. Read this book and learn from one of the best.

ANGELA KIMARU, executive pastor, Mavuno Church

Oscar lives and breathes the principles in *Seed It Out* in his ministry and leadership. Filled with practical wisdom from a pastor and leader who is investing his life in seeing others grow and flourish, it's a helpful tool for anyone who wants to invest in their own leadership in order to see others grow.

RICH GRANT, lead pastor, Alive Church, Gateshead, UK

Oscar Amisi is not just a leader; he's a developer of leaders. In this book he teaches key leadership principles that will not only inspire but also move leaders to be transformed into developers of leaders. *Seed It Out* is more than a leadership book; it is a guide to becoming an effective leader. Apply the principles in this book, and your leadership will grow beyond what you ever believed was possible!

JOSH WHITEHEAD, executive pastor of ministries,
Faith Promise Church

This is a much-needed book by Rev. Oscar. He demystifies leadership and shares practical truths in a simplified way without being simplistic. *Seed It Out* tackles leadership from a kingdom perspective. Rev. Oscar has challenged us to shift our mindsets from leadership that seems largely self-serving to servant leadership that goes beyond the clichés and calls us to live and lead by serving.

ALBERT SHITAKWA, pastor, Hebron City, Nairobi

The first time I met Pastor Oscar, I knew he was a natural born servant leader. I was so impressed at the way he could execute a huge vision but also love and care for each individual person that he came in contact with. Some people you meet come and go, but Pastor Oscar left seeds in my heart that have affected my life. As I read this book, my concept of effective leadership went to a whole new level. Pastor Oscar has a way of captivating the reader and drawing us higher. He writes in a way that is practical yet powerful. Every person aspiring to be an effective leader needs to read the truths discussed in this book. *Seed It Out* will empower leaders from every generation to grow in confidence to raise others up and develop them to be the best leaders they can be.

ALISON LUSTED, founder and CEO, CrossPoint Ministries

I have known Pastor Oscar Amisi for a number of years, and he has always been passionate about leadership and mentorship. This book is derived from his personal life journey as a leader and is punctuated with nuggets of practical wisdom, as he takes a vulnerable approach from his own experiences. *Seed It Out* is an easy and enjoyable read for anyone who is involved or interested in leadership at any level. I highly recommend it as a useful tool in leadership development.

REV. JESSE MWAI, CITAM

Seed It Out is a testament of Oscar Amisi's life mission: to leave a legacy of intergenerational leadership for the church, our nation, and the world at large. Oscar's vast experience and knowledge in leadership allows *Seed It Out* to blow a refreshing wind of change and ushers in a spring of fresh waters into Africa's biggest drought: leadership. The practical and tangible solutions in this book provide hope and direction out of our leadership crisis.

REV. NICK KORIR, senior pastor, Nairobi Chapel

This is a must-read for everyone in leadership. Whether you're in an executive position or not, the wisdom and practical application of the content will transform your approach to leadership. This is a resource that every leader needs to have in their toolkit.

NICK HINDLE, pastor, Influencers Church, Atlanta

Leadership in our generation seems like it's just about position, power, and privilege. In *Seed It Out*, Oscar Amisi pens down key fundamentals of what leadership is about, not just by definition but also in a simple, clear, yet profound way, unpacking the ageless principles of the core of leadership. Thousands of books have been written on this subject and one wonders is there something still to be written; yet, revelation is progressive, and Oscar—being an amazing leader himself and leading over years and across generations—has poured his heart and mind into this project.

This book is a handbook and tool every leader must read

and use to check their heart, role, and effectiveness as a leader. I highly recommend this book and believe it will be a blessing to you and your teams.

MUNATSI SANDE, pastor; author; life coach, South Africa

The African continent is experiencing growth, cultural transitions, and urbanization beyond any other time and place in history. The need for courageous and servant leaders in church and society are enormous. This is exactly what Pastor Oscar Amisi aims at in this book. Based on many years of experience as a pastor and leader, he shares his insight and wisdom on leadership that is built to last. Knowing Pastor Oscar from ministry partnership in M28, I highly recommend this book for anyone who wants to grow in leadership that serves both the church and society.

KELD DAHLMANN, international pastor; consultant and catalyst, M28; team leader, Kirke Planter Network, Denmark

I have seen firsthand Oscar embody the messages held in this book. He is a servant leader, who forms, equips, and empowers others. The ideas found in these pages are expressed in Oscar's everyday life and leadership; they are not just concepts but living testimonies that can inspire us all to become stronger leaders and raise up generations of new leaders.

RICH ROBINSON, cofounder, Movement Leaders Collective; cofounder, Creo

SEED
IT
OUT

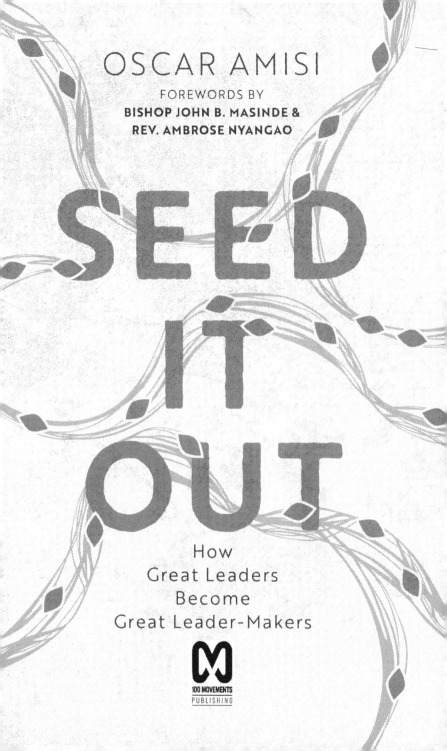

OSCAR AMISI

FOREWORDS BY
**BISHOP JOHN B. MASINDE &
REV. AMBROSE NYANGAO**

SEED IT OUT

How
Great Leaders
Become
Great Leader-Makers

100 MOVEMENTS
PUBLISHING

First published in 2023 by 100 Movements Publishing
www.100Mpublishing.com
Copyright © 2023 by Oscar Amisi

The author has no responsibility for the persistence or accuracy of URLs for external or third-party internet websites referred to in this book, and does not guarantee that any content on such websites is, or will remain, accurate or appropriate.

Some names have been changed to protect the privacy of individuals and organizations.

All Scripture quotations, unless otherwise indicated, are taken from the Holy Bible, New International Version®, NIV®. Copyright ©1973, 1978, 1984, 2011 by Biblica, Inc.™ Used by permission of Zondervan. All rights reserved worldwide. www.zondervan.com The "NIV" and "New International Version" are trademarks registered in the United States Patent and Trademark Office by Biblica, Inc.™

Scripture quotations marked God's Word are taken from *God's Word*®. © 1995 God's Word to the Nations. Used by permission of Baker Publishing Group.

Scripture quotations marked KJV are from the King James Version. Public domain.

Scripture quotations marked MSG are taken from THE MESSAGE, copyright © 1993, 2002, 2018 by Eugene H. Peterson. Used by permission of NavPress. All rights reserved. Represented by Tyndale House Publishers, Inc.

Scripture quotations marked NLT are taken from the *Holy Bible*, New Living Translation, copyright ©1996, 2004, 2015 by Tyndale House Foundation. Used by permission of Tyndale House Publishers, Carol Stream, Illinois 60188. All rights reserved.

Scripture quotations marked NASB are taken from the (NASB®) New American Standard Bible®, Copyright © 1960, 1971, 1977, 1995, 2020 by The Lockman Foundation. Used by permission. All rights reserved. lockman.org

ISBN 978-1-955142-42-7 (print)
ISBN 978-1-955142-43-4 (ebook)

Cover design and interior illustrations: Jude May
Cover image © KatyaKatya, Art Stocker | Adobe Stock images

100 Movements Publishing
An imprint of Movement Leaders Collective
Cody, Wyoming
www.movementleaderscollective.com

This book is dedicated to my daughter, Kristi Amisi, whose leadership potential and passion to serve continues to be evident as she grows up; and to the many leaders globally who are passionate about leading with legacy in mind and unlocking the potential of the next generation.

The future rests in the arms of leaders who understand that leadership is not about holding positions and hoarding power but instead is about empowering others.

May you be the torch bearers who pass on the light of impactful leadership to the next generation.

Contents

Foreword

BISHOP JOHN B. MASINDE

*Founder and Senior Pastor, Deliverance
Church Umoja, Nairobi, Kenya*

Leadership made simple. That is what *Seed It Out* is all about. Many of us have heard the saying from John Maxwell that, "Everything rises and falls on leadership."[1] It means that the kind of leadership you provide in any situation you find yourself in will determine the success or failure of that institution.

The kind of leadership necessary for you to succeed is not a mystery. That is what this book is all about. In five highly charged chapters, Rev. Oscar Amisi shares from his own experience and studies on how to give your leadership style a reality check and discover the heart, the art, the health, and the heritage of effective leadership.

I highly recommend this book to everyone aspiring to be a successful leader in any sphere of life. Read on, and you may be able to, "seed it out" to every generation.

Foreword

REV. AMBROSE NYANGAO
Senior Pastor, Parklands Baptist Church, Nariobi, Kenya

We live in an age where true and honorable leadership is scarce. There is so much material on leadership, and yet we do not have leaders who are making a positive impact—especially church leaders. Oscar Amisi has written an amazing book, suggesting that *we* be a solution to the challenges that leaders and leadership face as a whole. Writing with wisdom, he both portrays the reality leaders face and, through the reflections in every chapter, enables the reader to understand a better way.

Leaders are called to serve. Leaders must have a vision. Leaders are empowered from above to make a difference. Leaders must be positive examples in all that they say and do. *Seed It Out* will indeed raise a new generation of leaders who will advance the kingdom of God and its values far and wide. Get ready to be enlightened and impacted.

Introduction

Leadership is one of the most talked about yet least understood subjects. In the words of author and pastor Dr. John Stanko, we have "too many leaders but too little leadership."[1] My passion for writing this book stemmed from the firm conviction that when a generation has better leaders, everything in society becomes better. In this book, I will strive to paint a picture of what effective Christlike leadership looks like and how we can strategically recalibrate ourselves to be leaders that deliver.

I define leadership as:

a heart disposition that ignites a desire to serve selflessly, connect empathetically, and guide wisely.

Contrary to this definition, much of what we call leadership is nothing but glorified bossiness. In this book, you will find leadership principles that will challenge you to reimagine leadership and awaken the courage to swim upstream to become an effective, enduring leader.

You will realize that true leadership takes courage. Only

fearful leaders swim with the current of the status quo. Old wisdom tells us the majority of people follow already created trails, but true leaders have the guts to challenge the status quo, raise the standards, and boldly blaze new trails.

In my many years of leading in different contexts, studying leadership, and following effective leaders, I have concluded that great leaders do four things:

- **Serve:** They live to serve, and they lead by serving.
- **Envision:** They create clarity, alignment, and inspiration that inspires people to move forward.
- **Empower:** They demonstrate a mastery of empathy and a high value for human dignity.
- **Display:** They strive to make legacy-conscious decisions that create an impact that continues long after they have left the scene.

Missiologist Alan Hirsch says, "In every seed is the potential for a tree, and in every tree is the potential for a forest, but the potential is all contained in the initial seed."[2] A seed in and of itself bears exponential potential. However, a seed left to itself does not do much unless it is sown to the ground by the farmer. This process of ploughing the ground then sowing the seed in the right conditions triggers the possibility of the seed becoming a forest.

In the same way, *Seed It Out* challenges leaders to not just work to become better leaders but to also be great leader-makers by intentionally sowing seeds of leadership in potential leaders.

In doing so, they build a forest of godly leaders around them who have a kingdom mindset and are committed to transforming their spheres for God.

Leaders who "seed it out" leverage a kingdom-centered influence to drive the multiplication of emerging leaders and the establishment of a healthy culture that fosters integrity and societal transformation.

Every leader has the potential to be a "seed it out" leader. To turn this potential to reality, the leader must become self-aware, visionary, and selfless. They must know themselves well enough to know how they can be a resource to others; they must be visionary enough to see potential in others; and they must be selfless enough to give of themselves and their resources to facilitate the emergence of fresh leaders. This is what "seed it out" leadership is all about.

Seed It Out is designed to be a leadership empowerment tool to spur leaders to not only commit to being great leaders but to also be great leader-makers; leaders who "seed out" what God has put in them and who invest in raising new leaders and who operate with nimble minds and sharp competence.

The leadership principles I share in this book are drawn from lessons I have picked up on my journey of leadership, both in the church and in the corporate world.

I have been privileged to work in the trenches of youth leadership as a local church youth pastor for over fifteen years, as well as contribute to various global youth networks that have been at the forefront of evangelizing and discipling the current generation. As a church youth pastor, I started a leadership incubator known as the Doulos leadership experience, an initiative aimed at discipling and developing gap-year young people for leadership. Over 1,500 young people have gone through this experience, with many of them going on to take leadership positions in the church, marketplace, and political sphere.

Currently, I serve as the senior associate pastor at Deliverance Church Umoja, a multisite church in the heart of Nairobi, Kenya with a congregation of over eight thousand members. I also lead M28, a network that equips pastors and leaders to entrench discipleship and leadership development in their church culture.

These roles and experiences—in the good and bad, the highs and lows, the successes and failures—have shaped and stretched my leadership philosophy, which is summarized in the following chapters. This book contains the lessons and principles I wish I had known when I was first starting my leadership journey.

By the time you have read this book, I hope you will understand that leadership is not about visibility, bossiness, or charisma; rather, it is about a heart that serves Jesus and others, and a hand that adds value. You will be equipped, empowered, and enriched with leadership insights that will enable you to serve with purposefulness and lead with distinction.

REALITY CHECK
Character Before Competency

You can lead without character, but it's character
that gives you the moral authority to lead.
ANDY STANLEY

During my third year of theological college, we began preparing for an internship. This internship was a critical component of our training, as it was a prerequisite for graduation, and no one was taking any chances with it. Our lecturers even organized classes specifically designed to take us through the dos and don'ts to try to minimize any unnecessary mistakes.

> "Leadership is about functional
> servanthood, not status or position."

In order to get the relevant experience, we were given the choice to either go back to our sending (home) church or select another church. Either way, the idea was to put into practice the skills we had learned at college, whether that was homiletics (the art of preaching) or hermeneutics (the science of interpreting Scripture) or anything else.

Needless to say, none of us could wait to showcase our prowess. This was the moment we had been waiting for; the world would get to see just how gifted we were. It may sound a little melodramatic, but I felt a little like a soccer player about to play their first big match. After months of training in an academy, the player finally gets the chance to show people their skills on the big pitch. In my case, however, I would be demonstrating my fiery sermons and insightful teachings. The world was my oyster, and I couldn't wait to conquer it. My big moment was finally here!

With barely contained excitement, I chose to go back to my home church, armed with college documents addressed to my senior pastor that clearly outlined the expectations of the internship. With no time to waste, I confidently walked into his office one morning, with said letters in hand. After we exchanged greetings, I took him through my experience at the college, updated him on my education, and then—with chest puffed out with pride—I made the big and most important announcement: "I am here for my internship, the practicals."

"Leadership that has not been tested should never be trusted."

My senior pastor, Bishop Dr. J. B. Masinde, however, seemed to have missed the memo. He wasn't exactly falling over himself to give me accolades or to show me where to impart my very important knowledge. There were a few minutes of silence as he keenly went through my documents. Determined not to let my excitement wane, I firmly reminded myself that this was my opportunity to step into the pulpit and demonstrate my ability; and the letter he was reading, which had been personally addressed to him, was a testament to that fact.

After what seemed like a very long time, he asked, "So what do they expect you to do during your internship?"

Excuse me? What do they expect me to do during my internship? What sort of a question was that? Didn't the letter he had just read detail exactly what I was supposed to do? Didn't he recognize my gift? Was my faith being tested even before stepping into the pulpit?

With more questions in my mind than answers, and a need to impress this man who stood between me and my stadium moment, I cleared my throat and answered, "To teach and preach in order to practice what I have learned!"

Little did I know the response that awaited me. He asked me a question that has forever remained etched in my mind. Though I didn't know it at the time, it would be a question that would continue to shape my philosophy of leadership and still informs the way I lead to this day.

"Oscar, are they training you to be a preacher or a servant?"

> "You can't learn to serve in class; you
> learn servanthood by serving."

To this day, whenever I'm asked to talk about a major light bulb moment in my life, this tops the list. I did not have an answer. I mumbled a few words, but no coherent answer was forthcoming. When he noticed just how flummoxed I was, he quickly summoned one of the main janitors to his office.

In the coming weeks, I would learn a valuable lesson, a lesson I could never learn from all the years of pursuing my bachelor's degree in college. Don't get me wrong; I value the education I received in college, but what I learned practically in my few weeks of internship was something I would have never learned in any classroom setting.

You see all those years in college I was taught how to *do* but never how to *become*. When the janitor came into the office that day, he was instructed to supervise me as I did janitorial duties around the church compound for my entire internship. And just like that, my big stage moment dream vanished into thin air. Or so I thought.

Although it was a humbling experience, I remain extremely grateful for those janitorial duties because they gave me an opportunity to learn firsthand that character is the foundation of great leadership; servanthood precedes any bigger leadership stage. Learning how to model godly character by serving people put me in touch with reality. I learned that it's not the person who commands the big stage who is great, but the one who serves! Christ says, "The greatest among you should be like the youngest, and the one who rules like the one who serves" (Luke 22:26).

In the midst of that experience, I learned the following lessons:

- My identity and self-worth do not come from what I do but from who I am in Christ.
- My greatest impact does not come from platform expressions but from leading a life that is an example worth emulating.
- Leadership flows from who I am in private and not what I do in public.

"Leadership is about confronting your fears and embracing your possibilities."

Unbeknownst to me, this experience would set me up for the future challenges I would face in my leadership journey, especially in my initial years of leading as a youth pastor in our church. The experience played a critical role in molding my character and my perception of great leadership. I learned firsthand that serving intentionally as a leader is the best weapon in influencing even the most difficult and indifferent group of people, and it earns you their permission to lead them.

MOVING FROM LEADERSHIP BY POSITION
TO LEADERSHIP BY PERMISSION

My senior pastor once told me, "Leading is not a walk in the park. Servanthood gives you permission to lead; I can give you a position, but you will have to work to gain their trust and permission to lead them." That statement from my senior pastor still rings loud in my mind to this day. I did not understand it then, but now as a more mature leader, it makes a lot of sense to me.

> *"Leadership is about working on relationships, not barking orders."*

When I was first appointed the youth pastor in our church, I felt a mixture of fear and excitement for the task ahead. The offer of the position was unexpected, and I couldn't help wondering if I was the right fit, if I was ready, and if it was God's will.

Despite my fears, I took the job and quickly realized that being a youth pastor was no smooth sailing. There was absolutely no cruising, and the ride was the bumpiest I'd ever been on. The existing leadership had been running stuff for years without a youth pastor, and I imagine this development wasn't exactly exciting for them either. As a result, many of the staff were suspicious of me and my intentions, concerned I had come to interfere with the status quo.

After a while, it all became too much, and it was clear that several individuals were out to frustrate me, so I escalated the issue to the appointing authority for intervention. I will never forget being filled with righteous anger, seated with my senior pastor, and recounting the horrors I'd experienced in my first few months of service. I expected him to furiously summon all those I'd mentioned, give them a proper dressing down, and finish it off with a "shape up or ship out" ultimatum.

None of that happened.

Instead, he served me a cup of tea and said, "I gave you a position, but it's your job to demystify that position by working your way to a point where the young people in this church will give you the permission to lead them."

> "True leadership is by permission not position."

He went on to quote a leadership expert who once said you must move from *leadership by position to leadership by permission*.[1]

That was it!

I'm not sure I even finished the cup of tea. It took less than a minute, but the lesson had sunk in. In *leadership by position*, people receive you because they have been told by an authority that you are their leader. But in *leadership by permission*, people receive you not because they were informed of your new position but because they have seen how you have served them, and you have gained their trust and permission to lead them. At this level, you lead relationally rather than positionally.

When I changed my strategy and started working on building relationships rather than barking orders, things started taking a different trajectory. Even those who were initially suspicious of my appointment became my friends, and they played a big role in my work as a youth pastor.

The greatest key to gaining the permission of those you lead is to lead them in such a way that you will transform and change their lives for the better. Great leaders are motivated by a burning desire to become change agents who inspire people to be the best versions of themselves.

When you lead relationally and gain permission, the possibilities of inspiring those you are leading to greater impact are immense. You have earned their trust and can provoke them to practice what you are modeling; and as a result they are able to drive change in their spheres of influence. They learn that rank or position can never inspire genuine change in people.

As a leader-maker, you are now driving change effectively rather than just projecting a position. How then do you become a driver of change as a leader and not just a position holder?

Let me share the inspirational stories of two young leaders, Alex and Cynthia, whom I have had the privilege of training in our leadership development process. They both understood the importance of shifting from being positional leaders to leading by permission, as they intentionally sought to add value to those around them. They understood that even though they were young, they didn't have to just be *targets* of change, but they could be *agents* of change.

BECOMING A CHANGE AGENT

I met Alex in one of the young leadership development hubs I was leading, dubbed Doulos. In Doulos, we would take young people through practical life skills trainings, and later challenge them to find an expression of their leadership potential in society.

Upon going through the training, Alex and his friends were charged with the responsibility of identifying a family in need and helping them initiate a sustainable income-generating activity. Alex mobilized human and financial resources and was able to set up a small grocery shop that went on to support the family he worked with for years.

That singular project opened new vistas of vision for Alex. He dreamed of participating in community transformation through offering humanitarian assistance and economic empowerment initiatives. He realized that dream by founding an organization called Twah JALi,[2] which translated in English literally means "we care."

Together with a team of like-minded individuals, Alex has gone ahead to engineer innovative initiatives that have touched lives and brought about great transformation.

Over the years, Alex has significantly affected society. He has helped crowd fund for various projects that have contributed to the transformation of his community. They have been able to offer free barbering and make-up classes to help equip individuals with skills for employment. He has also organized numerous events to promote peaceful coexistence between the young people in his community and the local police.

> "Leadership is formed in the incubator of responsibility."

His rise to leadership was inspired by the desire to be a change agent and not just a position holder.

In my work as a leadership developer, I have endeavored to challenge people to lead by first being change agents and not mere position seekers. As leaders, we must be able to see potential. We must help those we lead overcome timidity and challenge them to courageously step out and become value-adding entities in their spheres of influence.

Such is the story of one lady by the name of Cynthia. We were honored to train Cynthia in one of our leadership cohorts, during which she was inspired to start an organization that empowers and inspires women to take charge of their spiritual, financial, and economic destinies.

Cynthia is the founder of Jithamini International,[3] a non-profit organization that is driving societal transformation not only among women but also in the education sector by providing school uniforms to children from very poor backgrounds through an initiative called Back to Dignity.

Leaders do not wait for things to happen. They see a need, and they step up to make things happen. In my own story, and in Alex and Cynthia's, the underlying philosophy that motivated leadership was the fusion of a desire to serve with a desire to bring change. When we serve, it enables us to lead through influence rather than through projecting our position. Leaders must learn to serve first if they are to get the permission of those they lead.

SEED IT OUT REFLECTIONS

1. What words would best describe your current leadership expression?

2. What practical things could you do to expand your relational effectiveness as a leader?

3. If your position were to be suddenly taken away, what aspects of your persona and character would help you retain influence with people?

4. What needs around you right now might you be able to respond to with care? Who in your sphere of influence could benefit from your encouragements to step out and become a change agent?

SERVE
The Heart of Effective Leadership

But among you it will be different. Whoever wants
to be a leader among you must be your servant.
MATTHEW 20:26 NLT

There are many ideologies that try to explain what leadership is. For some people, leadership is about being the boss, wielding power, or seeking publicity; for others, it's a means to satisfy self-interest. As discussed in the previous chapter, leadership is a heart disposition that ignites a desire to serve selflessly, connect empathetically, and guide wisely. In my experience, at the heart of true leadership is the willingness to be a selfless servant.

Servanthood is the sacrificial act of adding value to others while provoking them to excel. It is showing those you lead that as their leader you are ready to serve them, even when it's costly, inconvenient, or challenging. In the words of Robert Greenleaf, a renowned leadership scholar, "The first and most important choice a leader makes is the choice to serve, without which one's capacity to lead is severely limited."[1]

> *"Servanthood is the sacrificial act of adding value to others."*

When you embrace the attitude of servanthood, you shift the spotlight from yourself as the leader, to those you lead—your motivation to lead goes beyond self-interest. The true measure of success for any effective leader is not so much in the number of people they lead but in how effectively they serve them. This is the essence of leadership.

Great leadership is not necessarily driven by the passion to simply lead. It is driven by a consuming desire to serve. You create an environment that provokes those you lead to be better than they are. One of your greatest goals is to help them be the best version of themselves and succeed beyond what they thought was possible.

Good leaders must be good servants. The words of Martin Luther King Jr. ring ever true when he said, "Everybody can be great, because everybody can serve."[2] Every time you choose to serve and pursue the best for others, you are actually releasing greatness in those you lead. Servanthood is greatness in action.

JESUS: THE MODEL OF PERFECT SERVANT LEADERSHIP

Jesus modeled to us what true servant leadership is. He demonstrated that servanthood was not just reserved for those at the lowest level of a hierarchy. It is not about position or skill but an attitude that every leader should have if they are to lead just like Jesus did.

Here is how Jesus modeled servant leadership:

- **Compassionate love:** Jesus' love for the disciples and those around him was unconditional, a love that moved him to serve to the point of washing their feet— including the disciple who would end up betraying him. Jesus chose to put aside the privileges of heaven and lead this way. Servanthood is not a gift we are given but a choice we must make to humbly add value to others. As we choose the way of servanthood, it has a ripple effect. When we serve, we inspire those we serve to also serve.

- **Creative resourcing:** Jesus was solution oriented. He never complained about the challenges he faced, but instead he sought solutions. When the disciples didn't know what to do with the hungry multitude following them, Jesus used the few available fish and bread to feed the people. He used available resources to activate solutions to challenges, turning problems into opportunities.

- **Calling out greatness:** None of the Twelve were part of the elite society. In fact, they were a team made up of people who had come from disadvantaged backgrounds. Yet, although society might have dismissed them, Jesus looked to call out their greatness. Servanthood requires divorcing ourselves from entitlement and title-mindedness.

SERVANTHOOD: THE PLATFORM
FOR GENUINE LEADERSHIP

Renowned scientist Albert Einstein is reputed to have said, "Only a life lived for others is a life worthwhile." Various documented surveys on how people want to be treated by their leaders always end in the same conclusion.[3] People want to be treated with dignity and respect, and to be able to contribute to the success of the organization.

Effective leaders realize that the only way to create such an environment is to model servanthood to those they lead—and to do so will require a paradigm shift away from worldly definitions of leadership toward the example that Jesus set. We will need to embrace a new leadership philosophy that says, "Whoever wants to be your leader must first be your servant" (Mark 10:43, author's paraphrase).

"Great servants strive to have reduced entitlement."

Today we see many leaders demanding to be served instead of serving. I believe countries, churches, and corporate organizations will only truly see progress when leaders see themselves as servants rather than bosses who lord their title over their subjects.

To become an effective leader, it's important to realize that some factors are non-negotiable. Without these factors, you will not be able to lead yourself or others effectively. In this section, we will discuss three of them:

- Motive
- Mindset
- Maturity

Let us quickly jump into these three key pillars and see how they affect our leadership effectiveness.

PILLAR 1: MOTIVE

Motive is critical to godly leadership. Motive can simply be defined as the inner reason that drives us to do what we do. To be an effective leader, you must always ensure your leadership springs from a heart full of right motives. American Pastor and leadership thinker Craig Groeschel once said, "People will follow a leader with a heart faster than a leader with a title."[4]

Leadership starts with a desire to see others become better every day; a heart motivated by servanthood, where your social status or position does not stop you from humbling yourself to intentionally serve those you are leading.

> "Leaders with right motives are motivated by the desire to create transformation."

Popular culture views this kind of leadership as a weakness, but in God's leadership economy, the way up is the way down. To quote the wisdom of Proverbs: "Mixed motives twist life into tangles; pure motives take you straight down the road" (Proverbs 21:8, MSG).

Courageous leaders who desire to effectively lead take time to examine their motives, asking themselves *why* they want to lead. Organizations the world over are going down simply because those at the helm got up there for the wrong reasons! Don't be a leader unless you are doing it for the right reasons.

What Motivates You to Serve or Lead?

Leaders who want to serve are motivated by a passion to see transformation. Their heart is consumed by an overwhelming desire to see change—positive change; change that moves people from where they are to where they are supposed to be. This desire is driven by passion and not position. Servant-hearted leaders see the bankruptcy and hopelessness of those around them. They are interested in helping those they lead to discover and realize their God-given potential.

> *"Leave people better than you found them."*

Whether you lead in a religious organization, a corporate setting, or a school, your assignment is not just to manage people and maintain the status quo. Your success as a leader will be measured by how much you have been able to positively influence their lives. Are those you lead becoming better than when you first found them?

Mother Teresa was someone who defied all odds to add

value to humanity, a woman who was internationally renowned but humble enough to stay focused on her mission to serve the very poor of society.

Born in 1910 as Anjezë Gonxhe Bojaxhiu, Mother Teresa grew up in present day Macedonia and lived to become one of the world's greatest models of servant leadership. Influenced by her father's death when she was only eight years old, Mother Teresa already decided to commit herself to a religious life by the time she was twelve.

Her journey began in 1929 when she arrived in India. There, she became a nun and taught at a convent in Eastern Calcutta. After twenty years of teaching at the convent, she felt a "calling within a calling" and left her position as headmistress to aid the poor.

Teresa moved into the slums, where she faced hunger, poverty, and homelessness. Despite the lack of equipment and supplies, she found a way to open a school for poor children, teaching them to read and write using sticks in the dirt. Her efforts didn't go unnoticed. A new community soon formed around Mother Teresa—with hospices, clinics, and orphanages opened throughout India. Within a few years the mission went global—becoming the Missionaries of Charity.

By the 1970s, the congregation was helping orphans and those afflicted by addiction, poverty, disability, old age, and disaster around the world. In 1979, Teresa received the Nobel Peace Prize for her work to overcome poverty and suffering.

Mother Teresa passed away in 1997, but her vision continues

to live on to this day, as the Missionaries of Charity continues to serve those in need globally.[5]

Like Mother Teresa, your goal as a leader is to show those you lead that you care about them, and you want to help them. This helps create an environment that demonstrates you want to serve and bring out the best in those around you rather than use people as a stepping stone to your next level.

This passion to serve and transform others creates a flourishing and healthy environment where people feel secure to work because they understand that their leader is not just interested in outcomes but also in their wellbeing. When the environment is healthy and individuals are encouraged to flourish, their commitment levels to the leader's vision rises.

When the environment is unhealthy and toxic as a result of the leader's selfishness, people will work to comply, but they will never be committed. You know those you lead are compliant rather than committed if they only do what you tell them because they have to.

When people are committed to the leader, they do things not because they have to, but because they want to; their trust level in the leader keeps growing. They have realized they have a servant leader who is passionate about them and wants the best not just for the organization but also for the employees.

When you get your people to this level, you don't have to ask for delivery or loyalty—they will naturally give it to you.

Patrick Lencioni in his book *The Motive* discusses two primary motives for leadership and service:

- **Responsibility-centered leadership:** A leadership that is driven by the burden and desire to take things on for the good of others. This kind of leadership is about what it gives out and not what it takes. It's about stewardship of people and resources.

- **Reward-centered leadership:** A leadership that is about doing things that benefit the leaders. Leaders motivated this way will only do things when they can see how they will personally be rewarded—it's all about them! It's about what they get.[6]

Checking your motives for leading, and confronting them, will determine whether you will lead successfully. Let's now examine two marks of leaders with right motives.

Marks of Right Motives

Integrity. This means you are serving from a place of authenticity. You are real at what you do, and there are no hidden cards under the table. Today, leadership across the globe suffers from leaders who come to the table with a hidden agenda. What they project in public is not what they stand for in private. Most people are able to smell and discern phoniness and fakeness from a distance, and you will therefore struggle to lead if you are not authentic.

Former US president Dwight D. Eisenhower was spot on when he said, "The supreme quality for leadership is unquestionable integrity. Without it, no real success is possible, no matter whether it is on a section gang, a football field, in an army or in an office."[7]

This was so evident during the impeachment trial of former US president, Bill Clinton. As charismatic and intelligent as he was, he failed the integrity test. He denied and then subsequently admitted to an inappropriate relationship and faced impeachment. What he was in public is not what he was in private.

Leaders with integrity are:

- **Value-driven:** They have developed core values that inform their leadership, which enables them to make the right choices in their leadership journey. They are transparent and mean what they say.
- **Self-disciplined:** They have the ability to do what is right even if they don't feel like it. This is what holds and supports their value system.
- **Self-aware and secure in their identity:** They don't lead from a point of ignorance but instead have developed a realistic self-image, based on gifts, strengths, personality, and weaknesses.

It does not matter how talented, charismatic, or competent you are as a leader; if you have no integrity, your effectiveness will be compromised.

Selflessness. The fourth-century ancient Chinese philosopher and writer, Tzu Laozi, sums it up well, "A leader is best when people know he barely exists; when his work is done, his aim fulfilled, they will say; we did it ourselves."[8] Good leaders will give more than they will ever get. We live in a selfish world, and this has not been helped by the number of selfish leaders all around us. You will find these kinds of leaders in the church, in government, and in the corporate space. Every leader who wants to lead effectively has a big choice to make, whether to put their own interests first or the interests of those they lead.

Leadership is service above self. This kind of leadership is driven more by the burden at hand and what it can give to help. Selfless leaders bring others with them on their journey of leadership, intentionally seeking to help, engage, and encourage those around them. Their goal is to create a conducive environment for other people to grow, thrive, and be productive.

Wrong Motives for Leadership

A wrong motive for leadership will drive you to do everything to gain popularity and acceptance while disregarding the most important values a leader should live by. You become dishonest in your dealings in order to achieve your goals. You throw all matters of integrity out of the window. In this section, I will share with you three wrong motives for leadership that I have adapted from Mike Breen's teachings and book, *Covenant and Kingdom.*[9]

Appetite. Leaders who have a burning desire for personal gain use leadership as a vehicle to satisfy their wrong appetite. This is a trap for many leaders.

Jesus faced this temptation when the devil challenged him that if he was the son of God, he should turn stones into bread; this came at his weakest and most vulnerable point, having gone without food for forty days. But Jesus resisted the devil (Luke 4:3–4).

Breen says Jesus submitted his appetite to God and his Word, providing an example that every leader should emulate. As leaders, it is critical that we surrender our motives to God and allow him to shape them for his glory. Maybe the starting point is to do an honest self-audit of what drives our leadership and then ask God to forgive and shape our motivation to lead. We will need to intentionally starve our wrong motives and fast just like Jesus did.

We discover two things we must do as we follow the example of Jesus:

- We must resist our desire to fast-track our influence.
- We must resist our desire for attention and approval from people rather than serving God.

Ambition. Leaders motivated by selfish ambition are insecure and always seek to prove a point to those they lead. Their talk is never about "we" (the team) but is always about "I" (the leader). Their driving motivation is about their glory, doing everything to satisfy themselves, rather than the bigger picture of the organizations they lead.

Every credit for the success of the organization is attributed to the smartness and vision of the leader, whereas every failure or mistake is blamed on the lack of commitment and disloyalty of the team. These kinds of leaders will always struggle. To this kind of leader, the *role* they play is more important than the *goal* of their organizations.

In Luke 4:5–8, the devil tempts Jesus. In *Covenant and Kingdom*, Breen says that the devil offered Jesus an easier way to extend his influence, but Christ's priority was the glory of the Father and not just his own.

We must guard against selfish ambition, which is driven by the desire to please ourselves rather than considering the interests of those we lead. When we lead from a posture of selfish ambition, we are more interested in what we can achieve rather than considering the interests of those we lead. Instead of valuing people, they become tools to get us to our desired destination.

Our driving motivation for leading should always be to make others better.

Approval. For leaders motivated by approval, it's not so much about the organization's vision and purpose but rather about how popular they can become. This kind of leader suffers from approval addiction, an insatiable hunger to be recognized and loved for everything they do. To achieve this, they will publicize everything they do for everyone to see.

"Leadership is about people, not popularity."

Luke 4:9–12 is a clear test of approval addiction. The devil tests Jesus in the wilderness, pretending to give Jesus an opportunity to fast-track his journey to stardom—all he had to do was agree to throw himself down for the angels to come and hold him so that he did not break his foot. It would have been a sight to behold; and would have made breaking news on all the major news outlets. His social media following would have increased exponentially, and people would have instantly believed and accepted him as the promised Messiah. But Christ was not seeking approval or attention—he chose to please God rather than please people.

Like Jesus, leaders must strive to please their Master rather than those around them, who change like shifting shadows. Like the conductor of an orchestra, we must turn our back from the crowd and show commitment to our single mission so that we are not distracted.

To avoid the approval addiction trap, leaders should focus on their identity in Christ. Your identity is who you are in Christ rather than what you do.

The apostle Paul uses the metaphor of a soldier to illustrate the importance of being totally sold out to your single mission and single Master: "No one serving as a soldier gets entangled in civilian affairs, but rather tries to please his commanding officer" (2 Timothy 2:4).

PILLAR 2: MINDSET

Once you have settled the issue of why you want to lead (your motive), then you are on the right track. If your motivation to lead is right, then that will be evident in your attitude, which is the mentality that informs your leadership philosophy. Let's now look at healthy and unhealthy mindsets for leadership.

Servanthood is first an attitude of the heart before it translates into an action. Attitude can be defined as a way of thinking that affects our way of being and doing. Anyone can outperform themselves in service, and even be recognized by society for their actions.

> *"Servanthood is first an attitude of the heart."*

Servanthood starts from a point of selflessness that maintains a posture of humility in wanting the good of those around you. That's why it's not first gauged by your actions but by the attitude of your heart.

Renowned author and leadership expert Dr. John C. Maxwell says, "The leader's attitude is like a thermostat. If your attitude is good, the atmosphere is pleasant and the environment is easy to work in; but if your attitude is bad, the temperature is insufferable."[10]

In my leadership formative years, I had a wrong perception of what leadership was. Of course, this was shaped by my inexperience and age at that time. I saw leadership as a means to achieve popularity, to get the best position in the room, and prove my importance.

I will never forget a moment in my leadership in the year 2000. We were planning for an end of year students' camp. I was so pumped up and excited to be leading one of my first big events as a youth pastor that I decided to take charge of every aspect of the planning and never delegated or even gave ear to ideas from the wider team.

I felt this was my big moment to prove I was good at my job and the leadership had not made a mistake in appointing me as the youth pastor. I insisted on choosing the venue, coming up with the program, and selecting the different activities.

We eventually left for the camp, and unfortunately things started going south even before we arrived at the venue. Our numbers were smaller than previous years, and the camp itself was not bursting with energy and fun in comparison to previous camps. The days dragged, and by the time we got to the final day, everyone was tired and couldn't wait to get home.

When we got back, we gathered as a team to evaluate the entire event. It was clear to everyone that the camp had not fully met our objectives. To my surprise, one of the lead team members had the courage to gently and humbly challenge me to take responsibility for some of the decisions I had made without involving the rest of the team or considering contrary opinions.

My unhealthy mindset and attitude were exposed—my desire to prove how good I was and my false belief that I had the monopoly of ideas. I had to change my perspective of what leadership was about. My attitude has changed, and I now realize that leadership has to be collaborative if I am to see any impact.

The end result was that my change of attitude created a healthy environment in which people were energized, and creativity was unleashed, which significantly influenced our team.

Marks of a Healthy Leadership Mindset

Servant leaders have chosen to be motivated by a heart that wants to see people move from where they are to where they are supposed to be. Let's briefly explore the mindset and attitude of servant leaders.

> "True loyalty is always a function of connection, not position."

Great leaders think people first, not position. These kinds of leaders have learned to move from leadership based on the position they hold, to leadership based on influence gained through the relationships with those they lead. When leadership is about relational influence, people are no longer following you because there's a title on your office door; they are not just complying with your orders out of fear, but instead they are giving their all to the vision because they know you have their interests at heart. They want to serve and fulfill the organization's vision.

> "Servanthood springs from a point of selflessness."

Leaders who prioritize people over position are relational in their approach. They win people over by inspiring them through their influence and not by projecting position or pulling rank. True loyalty is always a function of connection and not position.

Great leaders take personal responsibility. Taking responsibility is the highest mark of great servant leaders. If you are a leader, you are not only going to take responsibility for your own decisions and actions, but you are also willing to take responsibility for the decisions and actions made by your direct reports. That is the measure of every great leader.

Instead of going to war with his troops, as was the custom of kings in Old Testament times, King David chose to stay behind and ended up committing adultery with Bathsheba after spotting her from a rooftop. He would later try to cover his sin by having Uriah, Bathsheba's husband, killed in battle. However, when confronted by the prophet Nathan, David owned up, acknowledged his sin, and mourned for days over what he had done. David was far from perfect, but he eventually took personal responsibility for his actions. Great leaders not only share the credit when things work out but also take responsibility when things don't go well.

In today's world, with all the challenges that leaders are now facing, it is probably more critical than ever before to accept responsibility for your actions and for those who report to you. But, it is tough. It is hard for top leaders to know everything that is going on with their employees, and yet, someone has to assume responsibility. Sometimes, we don't even know all of the things that employees are doing and yet taking the job as a leader means that in your area, you accept the ultimate responsibility for yourself and for them. You can't pass it on to anyone else since there isn't anyone higher who can accept it, and you can't pass the blame back on to those who report to you since it is commonly believed that you as the leader are responsible for the culture you have created.

Great leaders think purpose first, and not just results. Purpose drives the greatest of leaders. The Free Dictionary defines purpose as "the object toward which one strives or for which something exists, an aim or goal."[11] It's the reason for which anything is done, created, or exists. An important question that every leader and organization must answer is, Why do we exist?

Many leaders and organizations fail when they evaluate success by looking at results and not how well they are pursuing their purpose. A successful leader is one who is able to provoke people to first identify their purpose, and then go all out to fulfill it; once that is achieved, then the results are given.

Great leaders help people realize their importance in the organization, and how they can align their personal visions to the greater vision of the organization.

By considering purpose, effective leaders coach those they lead to be self-aware so they are better equipped to fulfill their purpose. It's important to develop a healthy culture in which people are aligned with their potential and productivity so that people don't feel they are square pegs in round holes. If you put people where they are gifted, you help them fulfill their purpose and give them a chance to thrive.

> "Growth is never accidental; it is always intentional."

When people are properly aligned with their purpose, there are two key outcomes:

- **Greater synergy and teamwork:** When people realize their placement, they have clarity on how they can complement other team members.
- **Greater individual contribution:** Purpose then becomes the motivator for productivity, enabling those that you are leading to unleash their full creativity.

PILLAR 3: MATURITY

Once your motive for leading or serving is right, this will be reflected in your mentality, which will be seen in your leadership philosophy—your attitude. This then triggers a desire to grow your leadership in areas where you see gaps. You refuse to be comfortable and settle but instead keep working on areas that may sabotage your leadership and those you are leading.

Maturity is not an event but a process, and mature leaders are those who have embraced a life of self-examination and self-adjustment. As a leader, it's essential to learn to consistently reflect on your words and actions to see areas that are out of alignment with the truth of the Word of God. In 1 Timothy, Paul challenges Timothy to engage in self-examination and adjustment, as he serves the churches in Ephesus: "Watch your life and doctrine closely. Persevere in them, because if you do, you will save both yourself and your hearers" (1 Timothy 4:16). The verse draws the attention of every leader to the need of embracing a culture of self-examination and also warns us about the dangers of a lack of it.

Maturity is the ability to exercise control over emotions and to make sound decisions rooted in principles. Mature leaders are better able to serve those they lead because maturity creates relational stability, a positive culture, and a sound decision-making framework.

Maturity does not mean having everything all figured out. Instead, it's the desire of a leader to keep improving, and to listen to the wisdom of others.

> "Mature leaders are always seeking to expand their capacity."

Mature leaders are always ready to acknowledge other people's success. They realize they are not perfect and are willing to receive correction and advice from peers; they are not defensive when correction comes their way. Mature leaders have learned to entrust responsibility and delegate authority to those they work with by releasing more and controlling less. Their mantra is "high accountability and less control."

Marks of a Mature Servant Leader

There are certain qualities that mature servant leaders embody. Let us briefly discuss a few:

Secure identity. Author Jeremy Caris said, "Insecure leaders use others to make themselves appear greater. Secure leaders invest in others to empower them to become greater themselves."[12]

To effectively lead requires one critical quality: security. Without a secure identity, it will be impossible to lead, develop, and even retain people in your organization.

In the Gospel of John, Jesus washes the disciples' feet, but before he does that, the Scriptures say, "Jesus knew that the Father had put all things under his power, and that he had come from God and was returning to God; so he got up from the meal, took off his outer clothing, and wrapped a towel around his waist. After that, he poured water into a basin and began to wash his disciples' feet" (John 13:3–5). His secure identity enabled him to serve.

Every leader battles insecurity at some point in their leadership journey—even the most successful and prominent leaders. A leader who has not dealt with their own insecurities can be a danger to the vision of the organization and the people they lead. These kinds of leaders are always looking out to be served instead of serving. Their insecurities mean that everything and everyone has to focus on them as the leader.

"Insecure leaders want to control the people around them."

Secure leaders, on the other hand, have realized that they are not competing with anyone in the organization. They focus on the goal of the organization and helping everyone to achieve that goal to the best of their ability. Secure leaders know that the goal is greater than the role.

Secure leaders are not territorial or possessive and are not intimidated by people around them who look more gifted than they are. Insecure leaders will always want to control people around them, and because of this they find it hard to delegate. They feel they are the only ones who can do the job.

Secure leaders are able to accommodate people with divergent ideas; they give generously, and they strive to empower and lift others to a higher level. The table below highlights some key differences between a secure and an insecure leader:

Secure Leaders	Insecure Leaders
Encourage others	Sabotage others
Recognize greatness in others	Overlook greatness in others
Are patient with others	Get impatient when people err
Admit when they are wrong	Get defensive and justify errors
Rejoice when others excel	Get jealous when others succeed

People smart. Every leader who desires to lead must develop emotional intelligence—the ability to interact with people in a healthy manner. This means they have the resilience to navigate offenses caused by those around them. Those kinds of leaders are called people-smart leaders—leaders who know how to respond to people and build teams that will enable them to achieve their goals.

A people-smart leader is one who is able to motivate and challenge those they lead to be more than they think they can be. They are able to connect with them at their level and influence them to aspire for greatness as they help others discover their potential.

> "Mature leaders are people-smart."

Leaders who are people-smart have learned to develop their interpersonal skills. They have learned that it's critical to listen to others—listening not to answer but to understand—and they are able to ask insightful questions.

In his book *The Ideal Team Player*, Patrick Lencioni talks about three indispensable virtues that individuals hold, which make teams successful:

- **Humble:** focusing more on their teammates than on themselves.
- **Hungry:** a strong work ethic, determined to get things done and contribute any way they can.
- **Smart:** not intellectually smart but interpersonally smart. They understand the dynamics of a group of people and how to say and do things that have a positive outcome on those around them.[13]

Mature leaders have learned to grow in emotional and social intelligence, recognizing that their actions and reactions will always affect those they lead either positively or negatively.

> "Your actions and reactions will always affect those around you."

Mature leaders are always sharpening and intentionally growing in their ability to handle different people and to build teams to achieve the organization's mission and vision.

> "Leaders don't just see problems; they see beyond problems."

Progressive capacity development. Mature leaders are those who are endlessly striving to expand their capacity under God. Growing your capacity does not just happen; it's something every leader should be intentional about.

Mature leaders invest in perpetual self-growth. Author and pastor T. D. Jakes once said, "The world is a university and everyone in it is a teacher. Make sure when you wake up in the morning, you go to school."[14]

Mature leaders have a right estimation of themselves—they recognize both their strengths and weaknesses. As the apostle Paul writes in Romans 12:3, "For by the grace given me I say to every one of you: Do not think of yourself more highly than you ought, but rather think of yourself with sober judgment, in accordance with the faith God has distributed to each of you."

We all have areas in our lives that we want to change and improve. This change does not just come; we must prayerfully and intentionally invest time, money, and effort in self-improvement if we are to achieve our purpose as leaders. There is a gap between who we are and what we are to become, and if that gap is not filled by the Holy Spirit's work in us and by training, exposure, and equipping, it can derail our journey to effective leadership.

We are living in a world that is dynamic and constantly changing. We must therefore evolve with a changing world by developing our skills and capacity if we are to remain fruitful. This requires a personal development plan. This might involve embracing a culture of self-examination, as referred to earlier. A good personality assessment tool can come in handy in helping you identify your strengths and gaps as a leader. Opening yourself to accountability by inviting trusted people will help you receive genuine feedback, which is essential for healthy growth.

Mature leaders maximize their strengths, but they also seek to bolster the areas in which they are weaker through training and openness to learn from others. This learning, self-development, and exposure never stops. As leaders, we should never get to a place where we say, "I have learned all there is to learn." Any living thing that is not growing is dying. Ceasing to learn is like stopping to grow. When a leader stops trying to learn and develop themselves, they start to die in their leadership.

Problem solving. Mature leaders know that their work is not just to identify and talk about the problems and challenges that their organization is facing but also to come up with means and ways of solving them. Leaders are drivers, not passengers, so they know that if they don't come up with solutions, no one will. People will remember you as a leader either for the problems you created or the problems you solved.

We must be wise and courageous enough to deal with issues that arise. Leaders see a problem or a crisis as an opportunity and not the end of the road. They don't just see the problem at hand, but they see beyond it, seeing the opportunities and possibilities that the problem presents. Such opportunities for improvement and growth may just enable your organization to leap to heights it could never have if the problem hadn't surfaced. This is an empowered perspective.

As we wrap up this chapter on serving, I pray that your greatest motivation for leadership will be a heart desire to positively impact and provoke people to become better, and to pursue their purpose by serving them unconditionally. Leadership is not about being the boss or wielding power.

Conventional leadership thinking glorifies the leader and the position they hold, with the subjects expected to serve them to a point of almost idolizing them. Jesus Christ's model of leadership goes against the grain of conventional leadership. Great leader-makers go out of their way to serve and to model what serving should look like to those around them.

SEED IT OUT REFLECTIONS

1. What are some of the inner motives and persuasions that influence how and why you lead?

2. A leader's mindset influences his or her effectiveness. What are some of the empowering attitudes that you would associate with the effective leaders you know?

3. Mature leaders respond to issues as opposed to reacting to them. What has been your dominant disposition when faced with challenges, and what do you need to do to be more responsive as opposed to reactive?

ENVISION
The Art of Effective Leadership

Where there is no vision, the people perish.
PROVERBS 29:18 KJV

In the last chapter we discussed how important it is for leaders to adopt a posture of servanthood. Once we have understood our role as servants, we can then embark on the next step of leading effectively: clearly painting a picture of where you or your organization is going. This is an essential skill for all great leader-makers. I call this *the art of envisioning*.

In this chapter we will discuss the importance of having a vision, what it means to have a God-given vision, how to clearly communicate it, and how to select people to whom you can transfer the vision.

VISION AND LEADERSHIP
An old Jewish proverb tells us that "the blind cannot lead the blind."[1] In the context of this chapter, a blind leader is one who

does not have a clear and inspiring vision for the future. It is extremely difficult to lead people when you can't see the future you are taking them to.

> "It is extremely difficult to lead people when you can't see the future."

I love the 2019 movie *The Boy Who Harnessed the Wind*, which demonstrates how the power of vision can energize an individual to pursue a goal that looks almost impossible with all odds stacked against them.[2]

The film centers on the true story of thirteen-year-old Malawian William Kamkwamba, who is forced to drop out of school because of a crippling famine, which means his parents can no longer afford his tuition fees.

Kamkwamba seeks to further his education in the local school library, and during his time there he stumbles across an English language textbook, *Using Energy*, with a windmill on its cover.

The book inspires him to attempt a seemingly impossible task: to build a windmill that will bring electricity and water to his village. With no money and a skeptical father, Kamkwamba is fueled by a passion and burning desire to bring light (so that he can study at night) and water (which will enable his village to grow food so that they don't die of hunger).

Although his father cannot understand what his son is talking about, Kamkwamba is undeterred and remains driven by a powerful vision to see his village transformed. Eventually he constructs a windmill using scrap metal, plastic pipes, and tractor and bicycle parts. His windmill is able to power light and a deep well, so the farmers no longer need to rely on unpredictable weather and insufficient rain. Kamkwamba's vision in difficult circumstances propelled him to international fame. In 2013, *TIME* magazine named him one of the "30 People Under 30 Changing the World,"[3] and the movie of his story has been watched across the globe.

The good news is that every leader can learn and master the art of being visionary. Vision is not the preserve of a few select individuals.

Look and Listen

Vision is birthed in the heart of the leader through *looking* and *listening*. As a leader, you must observe the happenings around you. What are the needs, problems, and challenges that confront your immediate circle? Which problems are you passionate about solving? Every leader must become an astute observer of what is happening around them.

> "Give yourself to the discipline of observing what's around you."

There is something called the law of exposure, which essentially means that our minds think about what they are most frequently exposed to. Leaders who champion great causes and stir up the next generation are burdened by visions that are born out of looking at and listening to the problems around them and being willing to step out and do something about them.

As you look at and listen to the problems, the challenges, and the issues around you, begin to ask yourself, *What are the potential solutions for these problems? How would the world look if this particular problem was solved?* Approaching these issues with an inquisitive mentality arouses vision and births dreams.

Great visions are often birthed in the incubator of attentive looking and listening. When I talk about looking and listening and how it influences vision, I am reminded of the story of Dr. Martin Luther King Jr.

In 1955, King was leading Dexter Avenue Baptist Church in Montgomery, Alabama. On December 1 of that year, forty-two-year-old Rosa Parks was heading home, seated at the front of the bus. At that time, segregation was written into the law, and the front seats of the bus were reserved for white citizens, and the back seats were for Black citizens. So when the bus became full in the front section, the bus driver ordered Parks and three other African Americans to move. The other three obliged, but Parks refused.

> "Are you going to stand up?" the driver demanded. Rosa Parks looked straight at him and said, "No." Flustered, and not quite sure what to do, Blake [the driver] retorted, "Well, I'm going to have you arrested." And Parks, still sitting next to the window, replied softly, "You may do that."[4]

Parks' refusal to move led to her arrest, and as the news spread among the Black community, people were agitated at the treatment she had received but were also angered by the fact that Blacks had been discriminated against for so long.

"Great visions are often birthed in the incubator of attentive looking and listening."

Blacks subsequently began boycotting the use of the public transport buses, choosing to either walk or board African American taxis that were charging discounted rates. The impact was so significant that the bus companies made huge losses. The Supreme Court would later rule in the favor of African Americans, and the law that ushered in discrimination and segregation was ruled unconstitutional.

"Give yourself to the discipline of keenly observing the happenings around you."

Martin Luther King saw and heard the challenges his community was facing. On the importance of listening, King once said, "Your knowledge of truth will increase as you know; listen to the truth of others."[5] He listened in order to understand the challenges his followers were going through, which enabled him to develop a rapport with the people. Upon hearing what had happened to Rosa Parks, King proactively mobilized the rest of the Black community in non-violent protests to fight the injustice meted on African Americans. His listening and his vision led to him becoming the leader of the civil rights movement in the 1960s.

His vision of fighting against the discrimination of the African American community was inspired from paying attention to Rosa Parks' demonstration. Visionary leaders are always looking at and listening to what's going on around them—and picking up issues that stir their souls. This becomes the platform upon which their visionary engagements are ignited and conceived.

In his engagement with the Memphis sanitation workers, Martin Luther King again demonstrated his ability to actively listen to people's challenges and become burdened to do something about them.

Two Memphis garbage collectors were tragically crushed to death by a truck they were using in February of 1968. The city's response so infuriated the workers that over one thousand Black workers from the city's department of public works went on strike, demanding recognition of their union, a safe working environment, and better pay.

The police responded with violence against the nonviolent striking workers who were marching to the city hall to demonstrate their frustrations. King showed solidarity with the workers by joining them on March 18 and addressing a crowd estimated to have been over twenty-five thousand. He exhorted them to persevere with the strike until their demands were met.

King's active listening influenced most of the leadership decisions he made and thrust him into public service, championing the cause of social justice, especially for Black people and the downtrodden … a cause that eventually cost him his life.

Conceiving a God-Given Vision

The Bible is full of the stories of men and women who conceived godly visions by carefully listening and looking. God used their experiences to birth visions that would bring transformation and deliverance for their people. Let's look at one example of a leader in the Bible who conceived a God-given vision by keenly listening and looking at what was happening among his people.

Nehemiah was a high official in the Persian court of King Artaxerxes I in the capital city of Susa, which lay 150 miles east of the Tigris River in what is now modern-day Iran. Nehemiah served as the king's cupbearer, and his position in the palace allowed him to receive visitors from time to time (Nehemiah 1:11).

On one particular day, a few people from his community visited him, and Nehemiah questioned them about the state of affairs back in Jerusalem, his home city.

Things were difficult back home, and Nehemiah's friends must have been reluctant to share the truth, wondering if their answer would spoil their time in the palace—such opportunities were rare, considering they were immigrants from a country that had been enslaved by the king! They eventually summoned all their courage and responded, "The remnant there in the province who survived the captivity are in great distress and disgrace, and the wall of Jerusalem is broken down and its gates have been burned with fire" (Nehemiah 1:3 NASB). "When [Nehemiah] heard these things, [he] sat down and wept. For some days [he] mourned and fasted and prayed before the God of heaven" (Nehemiah 1:4).

Something was birthed in Nehemiah's heart. He was moved to weep, fast, and pray before God—and a burden for his people and city was born. A godly vision is conceived from attentively listening to not only what God has to say but also to those around you.

Nehemiah asked a question that every leader needs to keep asking, "What's the condition of the people and the city?" Their response moved him to action.

Alan Redpath was a well-known British evangelist, pastor, and author who was born in 1907 and died in 1989. He once wrote: "Let us learn this lesson from Nehemiah: you never lighten the load unless first you have felt the pressure in your own soul. You are never used of God to bring blessing until God has opened your eyes and made you see things as they are."[6]

A God-given vision is also amplified in our hearts when we take time to look and recognize the devastation around us. After getting permission from the king to travel home, Nehemiah went around the city to look and see for himself the extent of the devastation he had been told about.

He inspected the damage on the wall and the city, but this was not just passive inspection. In his book *Hand Me Another Brick*, Charles Swindoll notes, "Nehemiah went down through the southern part of Jerusalem and back up the west side to the fountain gate. When he came to the King's pool, it was such a mess he couldn't even get by on his horse."[7]

Nehemiah took time to see the extent of the damage that had befallen his city. It's after this active observation that he invited his community to join him in rebuilding their city:

> Then I said to them, "You see the trouble we are in: Jerusalem lies in ruins, and its gates have been burned with fire. Come, let us rebuild the wall of Jerusalem, and we will no longer be in disgrace." I also told them about the gracious hand of my God on me and what the king had said to me. They replied, "Let us start rebuilding." So they began this good work.
>
> Nehemiah 2:17–18

As Nehemiah's story demonstrates, a godly vision comes about when we actively listen and look at what is happening around us.

What does it mean to have a God-given vision? Here are three essential ways to identify when an idea is a God-given vision instead of just simply a good idea.

- **A God-given vision is big:** God will never give you a vision that will only last your lifetime; that would be too small a vision.
- **A God-given vision is impossible without faith:** Because the vision is a God-sized vision, you cannot achieve it without resources and connections. It is doomed to failure unless you move by faith.
- **A God-given vision points you to God:** It's for God's glory. It's never about satisfying your ego or building your brand; it's all about showcasing the greatness of God.

WHY VISION IS VITAL

"Where there is no vision, the people perish" (Proverbs 29:18 KJV). Great leaders are individuals who use the power of vision to challenge people to a greater awareness of the future. Vision is vital in leading because it does three things.

Vision Enhances Perceptivity

When a leader has a clear vision, their perceptivity and that of those they lead is enhanced. Vision allows a leader to clearly paint a picture of the future that inspires people and emboldens them to rise above fear, cynicism, and doubt. Vision empowers people to appreciate their current reality while at the same time maintaining their focus on the horizon.

It gives a roadmap that is clear and ensures people are not easily distracted. Their priorities are spelled out, and it helps them to disconnect from anything that does not contribute to the realization of that vision.

> "Vision empowers people to rise above fear, cynicism, and doubt."

Vision Clarifies Placement

When vision is clear and communicated well, it helps people to know where they are best placed in the organization to add the most value in moving the vision forward. Fuzzy vision leads to misalignment and improper placement of human resources, which leads to people being underutilized or frustrated.

Lack of vision can cause people to feel like round pegs in square holes. Envisioning is the process of knowing where people best fit so that their skills and potential can be maximized and fulfilled, even as they champion the fulfillment of the organization's vision. When they are properly envisioned, people realize that the goal is more important than the role. Teamwork improves because everyone sees the other person's participation, and this reduces infighting and power struggles.

Vision Strengthens Purpose

Proper envisioning ensures that those you lead find meaning in the future; they also get to understand their role in the bigger piece. They suddenly realize that they are an important link between the present reality and what could be. A sense of purpose results in momentum that enables individuals to withstand every obstacle to achieve a set goal. A compelling vision of what could be brings excitement and enthusiasm to the team.

> "A compelling vision often brings excitement and enthusiasm."

A vision clearly articulated makes even the skeptical team member want to be part of something bigger than themselves. The picture of what could be makes them summon their last energy to make it happen. The table below compares the effect of visionary versus non-visionary leaders.

Visionary Leaders	Non-Visionary Leaders
Create clarity and conciseness	Create confusion and frustration
Create stability	Create instability
Create growth and momentum	Create frustration and stagnation
Create a healthy culture	Create a toxic culture

We have seen how vital vision is for any effective leader. When we don't have vision, we end up groping in the dark, unsure of the desired destination. However, having a clear vision is not an end in itself. You must be able to communicate vision passionately and convincingly so that people are able to understand and run with it.

In the next section in this chapter, we will explore key methods to strategically share your vision in a way that will raise enthusiasm and bear kingdom fruit.

STRATEGIC ENVISIONING

It is possible for a leader to have a great vision and yet not be able to communicate that vision in a way that stirs people to respond and engage. To envision people properly, the vision must consist of several ingredients.

The Vision Must Be Clear

When it comes to the process of envisioning people, clarity is essential. Marcus Buckingham says, "Clarity is the preoccupation of the effective leader. If you do nothing else as a leader, be clear."[8] Clarity of vision is about the ability to communicate in a way that is simple, memorable, and precise. Consider God's instructions to Habakkuk: "Then the Lord answered me, 'Write the vision. Make it clear on tablets so that anyone can read it quickly" (Habakkuk 2:2, God's Word Translation), meaning that the vision must be so plain and simple that anyone can understand it. Vagueness and complexity prevent buy-in. Clarity and simplicity are the keys that make vision memorable and "buyable."

When you communicate with complexity, people often disconnect from the vision, and they find it difficult to connect with you as a leader. Simplify your vision by thinking about the context of the people you are speaking to, the language that best resonates with them, and the metaphors they most easily identify with.

The Vision Must be Compelling

If a vision is to get buy-in, it must be compelling. By definition, a compelling vision is one that elicits passion, provokes initiative, raises people's hopes, and energizes their faith.

When a vision is compelling, it stirs up the people and becomes like a power booster that pumps adrenaline into their system, awakening unusual resolve and a go-getter mentality.

Returning to the story of Nehemiah, consider how he shared his vision in such a captivating way that everyone came on board. They all worked tirelessly with one single purpose: to see the restoration of their city. He drew their attention to how bad the city looked, the shame it brought on everyone, and the fact that they all had the power to change the city for the better and restore the pride of the people.

> "People best support what they help to create."

The Vision Must be Constructive

A vision must communicate how it will bring transformation. People must be able to see that the vision will deliver solutions and impact society rather than just benefit the visionary. As much as the fulfillment of the vision brings a win for the leader, the bigger win should always be for the larger society.

In a world where many people tend to be selfish, it's common to find leaders at all levels who are only concerned about their own interests. In fact, such leaders will do everything to ensure that all they do benefits them and a few of their inner circle. These kinds of leaders have a narrow vision and are not long term in their thinking; everything they do ends with them.

This kind of leadership encourages domineering personalities, including in the church. In the church, the culture tends to be built around the domineering leader's personality; unfortunately, more often than not, their giftedness and personality becomes a justification for control and manipulation. The vision must be bigger than the leader, which is only possible with

God's help. A godly vision is dependent on God and impossible without him.

The Vision Must Involve Consultation

Recently, I was involved in spearheading an assignment that would have our church institute some changes that were going to affect our ministry operations and enhance our growth process. As I was at the center of driving the change, I needed to envision the team and get buy-in from them, so we could streamline certain operations that needed to be realigned.

As the whole process was unfolding, I noticed that the team was not as engaged as they needed to be. I observed persistent sparks of indifference that stifled momentum and strangled synergy. I had to take a step back to consider why these challenges were occurring.

One of my reflections was that I had not allowed them to input into the vision. Catalyst leader Ray Johnson once said that "People best support what they help create."[9] The process of envisioning people should be handled with wisdom and consultative engagement. After changing my approach and embracing a more inclusive strategy, the team bought into the vison and were motivated to implement it because they owned the process.

> "A vision with a constructive end
> impacts and benefits society."

Many leaders go wrong when they adopt the top-bottom approach, where everything is discussed and passed at the top level and then pushed down people's throats to execute. As much as mapping out the vision is the responsibility of senior leadership, you only get proper buy-in and effective implementation when you allow those you're leading to speak into some aspects of the vision.

The Vision Must Not Be Rushed

During the same envisioning process, I also realized that in my eagerness to move things along, I did not labor enough to prepare the team for the transition. The more I tried to push the cart forward, the more I received pushback from team members, and the more frustrated I became.

As I reflected, I realized I had tried to rush the process; I had made some inaccurate assumptions that made me steam ahead.

I had not taken enough time to listen to the team. Although I noticed some red flags along the way, I had ignored them and consequently didn't get buy-in from them. One of the main red flags that should have alerted me was their uncertainty. Most members of the team were lethargic, lacked motivation, and did not follow through on the decisions we made together.

I realized that when driving change or communicating vision, it is important to exercise patience. Good leaders give time for those they are leading to get on board with the vision, and so the process of envisioning people is one that must not be rushed.

"Vision is nurtured in the womb of integrity."

IDENTIFYING VISION-READY PEOPLE

Having a vision and being able to effectively communicate it is part of the first phase of success in the envisioning process. The next big challenge is how to identify people to whom you can transfer or entrust the vision: vision-ready people.

These are faithful, loyal, and responsible people who can run with your vision even in your absence. Knowing the key qualities to look for in vision-ready people is critical because you're choosing people who will determine the impact of your vision moving forward.

Success in leadership greatly hinges on a leader's ability to transfer the vision to people who can run with it. Vision may be conceived by an individual, but it is always fulfilled by people. A vision that can only be seen and understood by the leader dies with the leader. Any leader who aspires to lead successfully must learn the skill of envisioning people. He or she must master the art of taking his or her ideas and convictions and sharing them with those they lead until they become convictions in them.

Vision is a pearl of great price. Wisdom tells us that it is not smart to throw pearls to pigs. Here are four key qualities that a leader should look out for when transferring vision.

> *"Integrity is the foundation of all leadership."*

Integrity

The famous investor Warren Buffet once wisely quipped, "In looking for people to hire, look for three qualities: integrity, intelligence, and energy. And if they don't have the first, the other two will kill you."[10] Vision is nurtured in the womb of integrity. People who show an obvious lack of integrity often end up being liabilities to a vision. When you include them in your vision, they end up soiling it with the toxicity of their own duplicity.

Instead, you should look for people who have integrity because they come with a value system that allows them to handle the vision with dignity. Before you transfer vision to someone or include them in the vision, you need to check their sense of discipline and integrity. They need a value system based on the Bible and need to model a high commitment to ethics and righteousness.

Hunger

Those to whom you transfer vision should display hunger. Hunger in this context refers to a person who has a great passion to grow and is willing to take the risks that are required for growth in vision. When a leader passes vision to people who are apathetic and lazy, momentum dies.

You need hungry people. People who will take initiative to go the extra mile, people who do not make excuses, and people who demonstrate an undeniable self-drive. Hungry people are often dissatisfied and are always taking initiative in reaching out for more growth and greater excellence.

Humility
"Vision-ready" people should also demonstrate humility. Vision thrives in the hands of people who are willing to grow. But growth only happens in those who are willing to learn. These are people who are ready and open to learn from others, irrespective of age or experience.

> "Humble people have a correct estimation of themselves."

Humble people model teachability. They realize they do not yet know all there is to know. As a result, they take correction positively and pursue instruction passionately. Humble people also have a correct estimation of themselves. They think of themselves soberly, and, to paraphrase the words of Rick Warren, they do not think less of themselves, but think of themselves less.[11]

Self-Control
When transferring vision, you also need to look out for people who are able to manage their own emotions and who understand

the impact their emotions can have on those around them; people who understand they need to regulate their emotions and not project them on the people they lead. Vision is about people, and a person who cannot learn to exercise self-control will end up being a poor steward of the vision. Emotionally intelligent leaders are able to master their emotions, which allows them to treat those they lead with honor and respect, no matter how they as leaders might be feeling.

We need to look for emotionally intelligent leaders; these are leaders who have capacity and competency to deal with people, and who are able to build teams that help them achieve goals.

SEED IT OUT REFLECTIONS

1. What is your vision for your life? Write it down in a clear, compelling, and memorable way.

2. Who do you see around you who displays integrity, hunger, humility, and self-control?

3. In sharing your vision, where can you grow in terms of the four areas: clear, compelling, constructive, seeking consultation?

4. The value of a vision is in its transferability. What are you doing as a leader to transfer a clear organizational vision to those with whom you need to partner?

5. What is the current level of buy-in of the vision from your team?

1	2	3	4	5	6	7	8	9	10

Low buy-in   **High buy-in**

6. What will you need to do to enhance the level of buy-in from your team?

EMPOWER
The Health of Effective Leadership

*Before you are a leader, success is all about
growing yourself. When you become a leader,
success is all about growing others.*
JACK WELCH

In the last chapter we learned how to effectively envision—communicating a clear vison and rallying people around it. The next step in the process is to *empower*: stretching others by intentionally equipping and challenging them to implement the vision as you push them and cheer them on.

Envisioning without empowering is an exercise in futility because without empowerment, a vision exists only as an exciting picture in peoples' minds but never goes beyond that. Empowerment is an intentional process that produces leaders who are trusted, resourced, and connected to the culture and vision of the organization. When done well, empowerment gives leaders the freedom to lead for the good of the organization without fear of micro-management or mistrust. Genuine empowerment requires an intentional process that needs consistent effort and commitment.

Empowering others means that, together, you can see your God-given vision become reality. In this chapter we will be looking at what it means to empower others and why it is critical to our leadership journey.

Empowerment is a word that defines great leaders. Bahamian minister Myles Munroe would often say, "Great leaders don't seek for power; they seek how to empower others."[1] An empowering leader is one who provokes people to become better, challenges people to think beyond their limitations, lifts peoples' hopes beyond their current realities, and celebrates when those people progress.

The supreme example of intentional leadership empowerment is found in the story of Jesus and his disciples. Jesus gave away leadership by empowering his disciples so they could lead and function without his physical presence. Jesus took a group of twelve men who would be considered misfits even in modern times; they had no education, pedigree, or impressive credentials, as the religious leaders observed when they cross-examined the disciples: "When they saw the courage of Peter and John and realized that they were unschooled, ordinary men, they were astonished and they took note that these men had been with Jesus" (Acts 4:13).

The profiles of these men were not impressive; they were

fishermen, anti-establishment rebels, illiterate, and high tempered. But Jesus spent time with them and exemplified a lifestyle as he trained them. Jesus showed us the greatest model of empowerment—transforming people who would not have been picked by the contemporary leaders into some of the greatest leaders that have ever lived. The Twelve, minus Judas who betrayed Jesus, became fruitful leaders who established the church and continued a movement that transformed the known world.

Think of Peter. Jesus saw Peter's potential, even though his failures and shortcomings were visible to all. Peter may have been undependable, but Jesus persevered with the hard work of empowerment, and transformed him from Simon, an unstable reed, into Peter, a stable rock.

In Mathew 14:29, Jesus invites Peter to do something Peter had never done before that would forever impact his faith in God and characterize his ministry and leadership life forever: "'Come,' he said. Then Peter got down out of the boat, walked on water and came toward Jesus."

Jesus, knowing both how unstable Peter was and the potential he had of becoming a great leader in the kingdom, challenges him to do something that seemed humanly impossible but would later be his reference point in believing God for far greater things in his leadership and ministry journey. Jesus invites Peter to walk on water, challenging him to go beyond his current experience. Staying in the boat was his safe space, but it was also limiting Peter.

One of my greatest fulfillments as a leader is seeing those I have empowered and walked with coming out of their shells; going from a place of lacking confidence in what God could do through them to a place of identifying their God-given calling and living out their full potential.

Like Jesus, great leaders are always challenging those around them to get out of their self-limiting boats and walk on the many waters of their God-given potential.

"Empowering leaders see great potential in people before it becomes obvious."

Another example of a leader who exemplified intentional empowerment in our African context is the late Bob Collymore. The former CEO of Safaricom PLC in Nairobi, Kenya, was a celebrated leader because he was people-focused. He created people-centered solutions and products because people were important to him.

"Great leaders don't seek for power; they seek to empower."

Collymore never shied away from going into some of Nairobi's deepest slums, and he even financially supported gifted children in the slums to learn classical music—something that many considered to be the pursuit of the rich and privileged. Collymore would support these children by creating a platform to nurture their talents, raising funds to support their cause and giving them exposure on big music platforms to mingle with world renowned musicians, with the hope that the exposure would help them break the limitations of their poor background. This was the beginning of Ghetto Classics, a music program that intentionally sought to teach music skills to ten- to nineteen-year-olds. The program is based in Korogocho, in the city of Nairobi, Kenya, one of the biggest slums in Africa, and is currently supporting over three hundred young people. This program encourages youth from the poorest slums in Nairobi to join orchestras and even have the opportunity to perform at Safaricom Live events.

Collymore's influence inspired many revolutionary initiatives, such as Mpesa Academy and Blaze. His support for employees and the culture he developed in Safaricom created an environment in which people were happy to work. In 2019, the firm was voted the number one place to work in Kenya, beating well-known mega companies such as Google and Coca Cola.[2] And this people-centered environment also yielded positive results, with Safaricom consistently being the most profitable firm in the East African region.

When the working environment is healthy and flourishing, people usually repay that by working toward the benefit of the organization. Collymore is quoted to have said in one of his many interviews, "I would like to be remembered for

SEED IT OUT

more than my ability to grow shareholder value and increase profit."³

POSTURES OF DISEMPOWERING LEADERSHIP

In leadership, posture is everything. Posture is a state of mind and attitude that a leader chooses, which either propels or hinders the process of empowering others.

If we are to empower well, then we must work out which methods will negatively affect our empowering process. Wisdom says that unique situations call for unique solutions. We must employ working strategies and discard those that haven't worked for us in the past. It's therefore important that we identify unhelpful postures that have inhibited our capacity to empower and inspire those we lead toward effective leadership.

Below are some of the disempowering postures I suggest every empowering leader avoid.

Bossiness—Use of Intimidation

My simplest definition of a boss is "one who orders others around in a domineering manner." We are not to intimidate others so that they do what we want them to do. Jesus warned his disciples to steer away from lording it over others: "You know that the rulers of the Gentiles lord it over them, and their high officials exercise authority over them. Not so with you" (Matthew 20:25–26).

People are looking for a leader who is relational and empathetic in their understanding and unconditional in their love. Leaders who seek to make a difference must toss out the hat of a boss and put on the heart of humility. Jesus told his disciples: "Instead, whoever wants to become great among you must be your servant, and whoever wants to be first must be your slave—just as the Son of Man did not come to be served, but to serve, and to give his life as a ransom for many" (Mathew 20:26–28).

Selfishness—Use of Manipulation

Selfishness is the refusal to put others first. People can smell the phoniness of manipulation and selfishness a mile away. They can also spot a generous heart that is ready to give and to provide an opportunity for them to grow, learn, and make a difference. People resent leaders who they sense are using them. But they will offer fierce loyalty to a leader they sense has their best intentions at heart and is willing to make sacrifices in order for that to happen.

Leaders with a bossy tendency are manipulative and will always demand absolute and unquestionable loyalty to themselves. Such leaders believe that power and authority should only be vested in them and cannot be shared or delegated. They become highly insecure if their subordinates attract positive feedback from others. This was King Saul's problem in the Bible. He sought to selfishly hoard all the power and leadership platform for himself, and became jealous of David and his leadership potential:

> When the men were returning home after David had killed
> the Philistine, the women came out from all the towns of

Israel to meet King Saul with singing and dancing, with joyful songs and with timbrels and lyres. As they danced, they sang: "Saul has slain his thousands, and David his tens of thousands." Saul was very angry; this refrain displeased him greatly. "They have credited David with tens of thousands," he thought, "but me with only thousands. What more can he get but the kingdom?" And from that time on Saul kept a close eye on David.

1 Samuel 18:6–9

Selfishness can cause leaders to act in all sorts of manipulative ways. Leaders will find themselves being forced to change by revolution if they refuse to change by revelation. Revolution is when circumstances force change upon a leader, whereas revelation enables a leader to adjust and change because they are sensitive to changing seasons. Selfless leaders are willing to share their space, platform, and even influence with those they are developing. It can feel risky to begin to empower and set up people for leadership success, especially with younger generations that seem to be in a hurry to get things done without appreciating the process and pain you have gone through to get to where you are.

Conquering selfishness is not about blindly giving away everything to people of unproven character. It is the willingness to gradually trust and release responsibility and privilege of leadership as we help to mold and shape those we lead with the kind of character they need to lead well. Leadership is not about leading others from a corner office; it requires coaching others into excellence as you give them space to germinate their own greatness.

> "Leaders who seek to make a difference must toss out the hat of a boss and put on the heart of humility."

Deception—Use of Lies

As we have already explored in previous chapters, people are hungry for authenticity and tend to disengage with a leader who projects phoniness or hypocrisy, both of which are symptoms of deception. People want to interact with a real person who knows how to speak the truth in love and doesn't seek to impress them with lies. People want a leader who is real; someone who is the same in the dark and in the light; someone who has consistency of character and a sober sense of love and humility.

Leaders will need to be authentic embodiments of truth and realism as opposed to lies and idealism.

Isolation—Use of Bureaucracy

The last mental hurdle we must overcome as leaders who want to influence and empower is the hurdle of isolation. In generations past, the leader was the person who called the shots and had the corner office away from the other, "ordinary" people. Such leaders were insulated by a layer of bureaucracy, so access to them was almost impossible. However, younger generations often refuse to be influenced by a leader who is unreachable. Instead, they tend to want leaders who are accessible, available, and sociable.

As longtime professor at Dallas Theological Seminary, Howard Hendricks would say, "If you want to impress people, you can do it from a distance, but if you want to impact them you must come close."[4] In this day and age, isolation will be the practice of those who want to stay in a state of dwindling influence and diminishing leadership potential. If we want to empower others, we must be prepared to trade isolation for association. As people called into leadership, we must be able to get out of our offices and get alongside those we are leading, so that we might listen to and understand them.

Once we move away from the unhelpful attitudes of bossiness, selfishness, deception, and isolation, we will then be ready to adopt more positive postures that will help us successfully empower those we lead.

> "If you want to impress people, you can do it from a distance, but if you want to empower people, you must come close."

POSTURES OF EMPOWERING LEADERSHIP

Let's now look at four postures that will enable us to successfully empower those we are leading and developing. They might appear simple, but overlooking or ignoring them can significantly diminish a leader's influence.

Visionary

We discussed the importance of vision and envisioning for a leader in the previous chapter. Without vision, people will not know where they are going. Vision provides an inspiring picture of the future that births passion and motivation.

Affirmer

People want a leader who will affirm them. They are looking for someone with an eye for their potential, who will encourage them in the things they are doing well. This is a function of vision because people who have vision see the potential in human resources before it becomes obvious. Good leaders choke the weeds of mediocrity in those they lead by finding their seeds of greatness, affirming those seeds into growth.

Learner

The leader who will influence and empower today's generation will need to commit to continuous learning. They will need to be well acquainted with the trends, challenges, and ideologies of the day. Those who fail to do this will only see a decrease in their influence. I challenge every person who aspires to be a leader in this generation to learn things that are outside the scope of their interest and to grow beyond their comfort zone. This will help us to become well-rounded individuals who can more readily enter the world of today's generation and connect with their thinking, and thereby influence and empower them for the better.

Listener

Upcoming leaders are looking for leaders who will listen and develop conversations with them. The best way to create a platform for empowering and leading people is to start a conversation with them. As author Dr. Mike Murdock states, every change begins with a conversation.[5] I might also add that every worthwhile conversation begins with the ability to listen, and to listen well. Upcoming leaders often have brilliant, hidden ideas and innovations that can easily be unlocked if only we will listen to them and create an atmosphere that allows people to express themselves without fear of being judged.

> "The listening leader will end up being the leader that successfully empowers today's generation of leaders."

THREE KEY ASPECTS OF EMPOWERMENT

Leaders must put in place intentional steps to empower the next generation. When a leader intentionally moves out to empower those they are developing, they can be assured that the vision will be owned, embraced, and driven with minimum supervision.

> "Loyalty is a function of connection not position."

If you are to become an effective leader-maker, it will require you to consciously build that which will outlast you. This means you are always thinking about leaving a kingdom legacy, regardless of whether you work in a Christian ministry or a secular role. To do this in today's culture, you will have to go against the grain. Resist the temptation to be too focused on the position, and instead focus on the next generation. Leaving a kingdom legacy takes hard work and sacrifice and requires us to pour our lives into other people. The only way to do this is to empower a group of individuals who you can train to carry on with the vision God has given you to carry out.

To effectively transfer vision as a leader, you need to invest in others in three ways.

Interact

To empower others, you must spend time with them. This does not mean a passive act where you only afford them presence and proximity. It needs to be an active process where you make yourself accessible to those you are leading so that they can interact with you in your everyday world.

Spending time with those you are empowering creates connection; you cannot effectively empower if you are not willing to connect with those you are leading.

"Great leaders are people focused not power focused."

In his book *Amplified Leadership*, Dan Reiland writes, "A leader connects, cares and adds value. He never leaves the table without seeking to have made a positive contribution. This all begins with personal authenticity, and the greatest blockage to this kind of transparency is self-protection."[6] As you spend time with the people you are empowering, they need to see transparency, vulnerability, and inspiration.

> *"Impart vision to people who have capacity."*

Train

You empower and develop leaders by spending time with them and then taking them through an intentional training process. You want to transfer the vision to those who have the capacity to carry it forward and ensure that your vision outlasts you. In order to do this, those you are leading must have their capacity developed by training. This training should take into account five very critical and important elements:

- **Education:** What information do they need in order to effectively carry out the vision of the leader and organization? Give them access to all the information they need to become better leaders.
- **Equipping:** What tools or skills do they need to be

effective leaders? You invest in them, knowing very well that your fruit of investment will be seen in their contribution to the growth of your organization and their impact in society.

- **Experience:** What platform do you need to create for them so that they can gain as much experience as possible as they execute what they have learned? Give them the necessary platform they need to put into practice what they have learned so they can gain experience. This kind of training enables you to have an all-round approach in developing effective and smart leaders who are not just theoretical but also practical in their approach.

- **Evaluation:** How often will you sit down with your protégé in order to evaluate their progress and growth? Are they growing in their leadership and responsibility or are they stagnating? You measure what you value. This includes checking your team to assess whether they are a good fit for their current role.

- **Edification:** Are you ready to take time and recognize their progress and hard work? Always be ready to celebrate and give them sustained encouragement that will build their motivation. What is celebrated will be repeated.

"What is celebrated will be repeated."

Entrust

Once training has taken place, you give them a platform and room to execute what they have learned. Leader-makers gradually entrust more and more responsibility to those they are leading. To do this well, you must break down bureaucracies and red tape that may hinder them.

THE PROCESS OF BECOMING AN EMPOWERING LEADER

By maintaining the postures and key aspects discussed above, leaders can follow a simple and effective process that empowers those they lead.

The process works as follows:

Step 1—The leader discerns a potential leader.

Step 2—The follower demonstrates honor for the leader.

Step 3—The leader begins investing in the follower.

Step 4—The follower demonstrates humility and hunger in learning.

Step 5—The leader commits to helping the follower to grow.

Step 6—The follower cooperates and starts the upward cycle of growth.

Empowering others is a systematic process; it does not happen without intentional action. Leaders must invest time and resources if they are to develop, empower, and multiply leaders. In his book, *Multiplying Missional Leaders*, Mike Breen brings clarity to this process of empowerment:

> To be effective as an empowering leader, you will need a clear plan and process that will aid you in empowering leaders who embody the culture you envision for your organisation. This cannot happen by accident or be wished into existence, it must be by design.[7]

Various leadership authorities, both in the body of Christ and the marketplace, recommend the importance of creating a predictable leadership pipeline. A pipeline is a systematic process that enhances the development of leaders, training, and deployment.

In the Gospels, Jesus models a simple leadership development pipeline that was key in his training of his disciples. This is particularly evident in Luke 9 and 10. Mike Breen categorizes these in four progressive, reproducible steps that can be replicated across all cultures:

- **Recruit:** Jesus recruited his leaders when he called the twelve disciples to learn to be like him and to do all of the kingdom things he could do.
- **Train:** Jesus then asked the disciples to watch all the things he did. He took time to explain and break down his teachings to them and gave them opportunities to try out what he taught them with him by their side.
- **Deploy:** From time to time, Jesus released the disciples to live out what he had taught them. He sent them out on mission two by two to do all the things they had seen him do (Luke 10).

- **Review:** After they came back from their first sending (Luke 10), Jesus sat down with them to process and report back what they had seen and experienced.[8]

After the review stage, this learning process can begin again with the same group of disciples experiencing the train, deploy, and review process in a new context or experience.

> *"People want to grow in their leadership journey; no one wants to remain static."*

CREATING A CULTURE OF EMPOWERMENT

To become an empowering leader, there are three things that must be woven into the fabric of your leadership culture.

Trust

Nothing facilitates empowerment like creating a high-trust environment. Leaders can create a high-trust environment that supports the culture of empowerment by modeling respect in relationships. When people feel respected, they become more open to the leader's influence and input where their growth is concerned.

More importantly, a high-trust environment is where integrity is not just a value that is talked about but a value that is embraced and practiced. When a leader models integrity and a commitment to ethics, they inspire trust, and that trust creates good ground for the seed of empowerment to grow.

"*When a leader models integrity, they inspire trust.*"

People Development

A culture of empowerment has a high commitment to people development. To be effective people developers, we as leaders must change how we perceive those around us. Preconceived notions, perceptions, and biases about people, especially when we have not given them the benefit of the doubt, is a major hindrance to successful leadership development.

If we are to ever develop leaders around us, we must put on a new pair of lenses that allow us to see the raw potential in people. We must see people beyond who and where they are currently and instead see them as who and what they could become.

People grow through learning and investment, so as a leader, you must model a learning culture, as well as create opportunities for people to learn and grow. People need to see you paying the price to grow and advance in your own pursuit of wisdom before they can be inspired to do the same in their own lives.

Empowering leaders intentionally develop people from within their organizations as opposed to importing them from outside. Empowering leaders do not go outside their organization to get a finished product to bridge existing leadership gaps, and they realize that acquiring leaders in this way communicates to those within that they are insufficient and incapable of becoming distinguished leaders. To consistently go outside the organization for leaders instead of developing them from within is called leadership acquisition rather than leadership development.

As a leadership developer, you must offer potential leaders mentorship opportunities, and do everything you need to do to empower people to grow. A high commitment to people development is also easily demonstrated by how a leader treats people when they fail. An empowering leader encourages people to learn from their failures rather than be ruined by them.

> *"You need humility to embrace*
> *people who are not like you."*

Clarity of Growth

An empowering leader creates a structured growth path that clarifies where people will be if they grow. Most people want to grow in their leadership journey. Few people want to remain static and be at the same place, year in and year out. However, people are often not inspired to develop because there is no clear pathway that shows them what their future will look like if they grow. As a result, there is no incentive to engage in personal development and personal empowerment. Therefore, a great way of engaging and retaining leaders is to put in place a plan that clearly spells out their leadership growth path.

A great leader clarifies to upcoming leaders their future leadership milestones. By painting this picture, upcoming leaders are inspired and motivated to engage because they are able to see both the need for empowerment and the rewards that come along with it.

One valuable lesson I learned as I've sought to empower others is that I need humility to embrace people who are not like me. Empowering people is not about conforming people to my personality but instead is about transferring to them the empowering wisdom I have learned and empowering them to conform to Jesus.

The first time I worked with a group of interns, I made the mistake of assuming that my success would be measured by how much I had made them like me. I got really frustrated when they didn't handle things as I would. It took a lot of humility for me to get to the place of realizing that empowering is not about cloning people to your own image; it is about encouraging and empowering people to be all God has created them to be.

I had a misconceived perception of the empowerment process, which created lots of frustrations. I had to do a lot of unlearning and came to realize that when you are dealing with people who are different from you, you must adapt your style of engagement so that you can reach them within their context of understanding.

As I have continued learning how to best empower others, I have realized I need to be more open-minded and need to develop sufficient emotional reserves to allow my protégés to ask me hard questions. I have discovered that there is great reward in giving them permission to express their suggestions and to explore their creativity.

It takes tremendous levels of emotional intelligence for a leader to be able to discern the difference between creative expression and rebellion. You can only empower others to the extent that you are patient with them. Be willing to patiently engage with them, and don't attempt to microwave the process. Every process of empowerment takes time and demands patience.

> *"It takes discernment to differentiate between creative expression and rebellion."*

OUTCOMES OF STRATEGIC EMPOWERMENT

When empowerment is done well, it has great benefits. I would like to highlight two key outcomes when leaders invest in creating a culture of empowering others.

People are Energized

When people are empowered, they become inspired, and their energy levels are greatly increased. Empowered people are more passionate and more committed to the work of pushing the vision forward. Former US president Ronald Reagan captured it best when he said, "The greatest leader is not necessarily the one who does the greatest things. He is the one who gets the people to do the greatest things."[9] A culture of empowerment is the platform upon which people are empowered to do great things and become great people.

> *"Energized people often have high levels of enthusiasm."*

People are Engaged

Engagement speaks of doing something with next-level commitment. When people feel empowered, they unleash next-level commitment, regardless of whether someone is supervising.

Success for any organization is not just about the bottom line and expected outcomes but also about the welfare of those you lead. You must focus on helping people feel so empowered that they outdo themselves in terms of their engagement at work. When you truly empower people, they feel their goals are achievable, their work is worthwhile, and believe their contribution counts. Successful leaders don't just engage the hands of people at work; they engage their souls as well.

This kind of engagement makes them feel a connection to the vision of the leader and the organization that goes beyond personal interest. They no longer see themselves as just employees or volunteers but as co-owners of the vision. They know that the success of the organization is their success, and the failure of the organization will impact them too and not just the leader. Their commitment is a heart and soul commitment.

Intentionally developing a posture that helps you empower people has a high return on investment. It enriches organizations, enlarges vision, and maximizes possibilities of productivity. Any leader who is serious about the future must be consciously engaged in the process of empowering others.

Without leadership empowerment as part of your process of developing the leaders around you, the health of your leadership development will be greatly compromised. Instead of developing leaders, you will have developed followers.

When empowerment is done well, it enables those you are developing to always rise to the occasion while carrying out your vision. They are able to implement what they have been taught, and in the process are able to make critical decisions for the betterment of the organization. Great leader-makers intentionally choose to lead a group of other empowered leaders.

SEED IT OUT REFLECTIONS

1. How would you rate your intentionality in the empowerment process? What evidence is there of you currently empowering other leaders?

2. What is one way you can imitate the empowering leadership of Jesus in how he empowered his disciples?

3. What postures of empowering and disempowering leadership describe your current leadership mindset and practice? What is one posture you'd like to make progress in this year? Do you recognize any of the empowering postures in the young leaders around you?

4. Of interacting, training, and entrusting, is there one which is the most difficult for you to invest in young leaders? If so, what, and why might that be?

5. Think of a young leader in your life. For the six-step process of empowerment, at what stage are you currently with him or her?

6. Do you have a system in place for recruiting, training, deploying, and reviewing? If not, who can you partner with to activate that process?

7. Do young leaders in your organization have a platform to share their voice and grow, or are they dependent upon you?

8. How might you develop others to be more energized and more engaged in the empowerment journey?

DISPLAY
The Heritage of Effective Leadership

*Leadership is about making others better as
a result of your presence and making sure
that impact lasts in your absence.*
SHERYL SANDBERG

We have seen how empowering leaders motivates people to go beyond even their own expectations. When people are empowered, they make the vision their own—they are no longer in your organization solely for their own benefit, but instead they see themselves as shareholders in the vision. Once leaders are empowered, it is essential to intentionally create a platform that gives them opportunities to thrive and shine in their leadership journey.

We need to become "displayer leaders"—leaders who are prepared to fade into the background, creating platforms for those we have developed in order to execute that which they have been taught all along. Displayer leaders are leaders who create opportunities and open doors for those they lead.

There are leaders who lead followers, and there are leaders who grow leaders. We display mature leadership when we become *nurturers of leaders*.

> "Displayer leaders are opportunity creators."

PETE'S STORY

Pete joined the marketing staff at Xenia, having come from their chief rival, Zenox.[1] An award-winning marketer, Pete had proven himself competent in the regional market. When Pete joined Xenia, Zenox was the current leading marketing firm in the region, a position they snatched from Xenia, which had been the undisputed leader for five years in a row.

Using his aggressive negotiating skills, Pete had helped Zenox dethrone Xenia as the leading marketing firm. Every big deal and tender had gone to Zenox, leaving Xenia to fight for leftovers with other smaller companies. As a result, Xenia was labeled a fallen giant.

With a new chief executive on board, Xenia had gone out in search for the greatest talent that would catapult them to the top of the market once again. The new chief executive gave Pete a deal he could not resist, so he crossed over and joined his fiercest rivals at Xenia. The rivalry between these two companies was so severe that even the marketing executives hated each other.

Having previously been rivals, Pete's new colleagues at Xenia knew him well and felt uncomfortable working with the man who had snatched big tenders from them in the past. Pete was not welcomed into any of the small groups that broke for lunch and evening coffee together. He quickly realized he was going to have a tough ride in his new role and began to wonder if he made a mistake by switching firms.

After a couple of months in his new role, he still wasn't making any headway, and those who were supposed to facilitate deals he clinched were not cooperating with him. Meanwhile, the chief executive was expecting an avalanche of business because they now had the region's marketing top dog.

Bunny was another staff member at Xenia who had worked at the firm for some time and was well respected because of his people skills. He had moved up the ladder to become one of the team heads in marketing. Bunny had been on leave when Pete joined, so they had not officially met, though Bunny knew of Pete because of Pete's work with Zenox. After observing Pete, Bunny quickly realized that, unlike everyone else in the marketing department, Pete was going on pitching missions alone. Bunny offered to buy Pete coffee one evening after work. He was impressed by Pete and realized he was not the person he thought he was when he was in the opposing camp.

He decided to pair himself up with Pete for all their pitching and introduced him to a few people at the company. He even went a step further and introduced Pete to some of his own clients.

Pete felt relieved because he had found someone who was not jealous or threatened by him. Over the next two years, Pete not only learned from Bunny and excelled in his people skills, but he also started bringing the company businesses that had previously eluded them.

Pete began to catch the eye of not only the executive but also the board of directors. Colleagues began to tell Bunny that Pete would soon take up his position if Pete continued to rise. But Bunny believed they were all working toward the same goal, which was to help the company regain its lost status. Within five years, Pete had risen to the position of the top marketer in the company, but Bunny never felt threatened. Instead he continued to urge him on and chose to play second fiddle to the man whom he had introduced to their clients.

Bunny eventually reached retirement age and left the company, having not only welcomed Pete but having also laid a platform for him to thrive in an environment that was initially hostile toward him.

BECOMING A DISPLAYER LEADER

Bunny had the DNA of a displayer leader, so let's now look more specifically at that DNA. To become a displayer, there are three things that need to be embedded into your character and leadership philosophy.

Displayer Leaders are Platform Creators

Leaders who desire to make an impact and leave a legacy make a deliberate commitment to be the shoulders on which the next leaders will stand. Every great leader knows that they are responsible for creating a process for growth and the development of those they lead.

Be a door and not a ceiling. Displayer leaders know they cannot afford to be a ceiling that blocks and frustrates the growth and exposure of their protégés; instead, they need to be door openers who afford opportunities to everyone around them. A door speaks of something that gives access. A ceiling, on the other hand, is a limiting restriction that hinders something from rising. Being a door means you must perceive yourself as one who has been placed in the lives of others to help them access higher levels of life and leadership expression. You must be secure enough to not only share your platform with those you lead but also be willing to open doors that will grow their skills and give them exposure that will take their leadership to a higher level. Displayer leaders are okay with the fact that their protégés always surpass them.

Great leader-makers, just like Jesus, understand that one of their biggest tasks is to open doors of opportunities so that those they are developing can go through and rise into what God has called them to be.

Jesus was the greatest door opener that ever lived. In fact, in John's Gospel, he calls himself not just the door but the gate:

Therefore Jesus said again, "Very truly I tell you, I am the gate for sheep. All who have come before me are thieves and robbers, but the sheep have not listened to them. I am the gate; whoever enters through me will be saved. They will come in and go out, and find pasture."

John 10:7–9

Jesus not only opened the doors of salvation but also of leadership opportunities. He allowed his disciples to experience God's power at work through them, as he changed and transformed the known world at that time.

Contrast this with the Pharisees who were a ceiling, only allowing people to approach God through them, and obstructing those who freely wanted to access God.

Opened doors transformed the lives of the disciples and set them up to lead the first church. The doors of opportunity transformed Peter, the timid and unstable into a steady rock that would lead the other apostles. Matthew, once a loathed and corrupt tax collector, experienced transformation because Jesus gave him access to himself and to a great team. Jesus did not allow the disciples' present deficiencies to deter him from opening doors for them but instead focused on their potential for the future. Jesus believed that people change, and so he opened the doors and gave them a chance.

> "Displayer leaders intentionally give access to their protégés."

Create opportunities for people. It is one thing to be a door and another thing altogether to be an open door. A legacy-thinking leader goes out of their way to create opportunities for those they lead. They share the networks and opportunities that their experience in leadership engagement has afforded them.

I had a unique experience in my own leadership journey that enabled me to pivot to the next level of my leadership expression. In one of my training experiences, I met Colin Piper who at the time was the chair of the World Evangelical Alliance Youth Commission. Colin took a liking to me and created a platform for me to further grow my leadership by exposing me to other global youth influencers.

This exposure allowed me to gain access to networks and relationships that have since helped me to pioneer fresh initiatives. One of those initiatives is a learning community that has mobilized and trained hundreds of leaders in Kenya and Zambia. We have held workshops in Zambia and have attracted delegates from as far as Congo. All this came about because someone was willing to selflessly open doors and create platforms for me. As a result of Colin's selflessness, many other leaders have been able to learn about and implement disciple-making movements as well as ignite positive transformation in their spheres of influence.

Jesus created opportunities. He is our greatest example of a displayer leader, who not only discipled and developed a group of twelve men into powerful leaders but also set a platform for them to go further than he did during his earthly ministry.

Jesus picked a group of men that would not have made it to anyone's A-team today. Jesus is the world's greatest ever displayer leader because he was never afraid that his disciples would surpass him. He knew his purpose, and he was secure in his calling. He set his disciples up for success when he said they would do, "even greater things than these" (John 14:12).

This was more about quantity than quality, meaning that their scope of ministry would go far beyond where Jesus had reached physically. Christ's ministry was localized in Palestine, but the disciples went beyond Palestine. With the birth of the church, their ministry went to the rest of the world, to areas where Jesus never stepped when he was physically on earth.

> "Displayer leaders are secure enough to allow their protégés to surpass them."

These "unschooled, ordinary men" (Acts 4:13) wrote almost half of the New Testament that we have today. Their ministry and impact went beyond Palestine to Europe and Africa.

Jesus identified the next generation of leaders, trained them, gave them authority, and eventually set a stage for them to thrive. Let us consider four key things that Jesus did to display his disciples:

- **Modeling:** He modeled and allowed them to see his way of life: "He appointed twelve that they might be with him and that he might send them out to preach" (Mark 3:14).

- **Mentoring:** He taught the disciples and immersed them in the wisdom he carried. "The disciples came to him and asked, 'Why do you speak to the people in parables?' He replied, 'Because the knowledge of the secrets of the kingdom of heaven has been given to you, but not to them'" (Matthew 13:10–11).

- **Maturing:** He gave them responsibility that allowed them to do what he had taught them. He matured them by giving them responsibility: "The Lord appointed seventy-two others and sent them two by two ahead of him to every town and place where he was about to go" (Luke 10:1).

- **Motivating:** He gave them a high challenge and affirmation that they would do even greater things than the things he did: "Very truly I tell you, whoever believes in me will do the works I have been doing, and they will do even greater things than these, because I am going to the Father" (John 14:12).

Jesus enlarged the world of his disciples by encouraging and affirming them. Displayer leaders know that leaders don't come as finished products; they have to be formed, equipped, and displayed, allowing them to confidently execute what they have learned. Displayer leaders are intentional in letting those they lead feel their support; their leadership development philosophy is, "I believe in you," and they show this with both their actions and their words.

Displayer leaders intentionally work not just to be great leaders but also to make other great leaders. You will know that you are becoming a great leader when you enjoy watching other people grow and flourish, especially those whom you have empowered.

Help people sustain influence, credibility, and access. Any person who has engaged in leadership for a while knows that it takes endorsement or competence to open a door, but it takes wisdom to keep a door open. Sustaining open doors demands that a displayer leader lives with a sense of accountability. Displayer leaders know the importance of taking advantage of every opportunity to use their influence to give their apprentice credibility and access to their networks if they are to continue developing as leaders.

Legacy-minded leaders understand that just as continuous watering and fertilizing of plants help them grow healthy and strong, so too, networks and opportunities need to be stewarded with wisdom and discretion. These leaders not only instill this wisdom into their mentees, but they also afford them access to their own networks and platforms so that they can keep ascending healthily and maturely on the plane of leadership growth.

The apostle Paul was an effective displayer leader, and among the many he empowered and displayed was Timothy, his spiritual son:

Paul, an apostle of Christ Jesus by the command of God our
Savior and of Christ Jesus our hope, To Timothy my true
son in the faith: Grace, mercy and peace from God the
Father and Christ Jesus our Lord.

1 Timothy 1:1–2

Paul mentored and developed Timothy and set him up for
ministry at a young age. Timothy accompanied Paul on his
missionary journey and served him as an apprentice. Timothy's
progress and development as a leader is evident in the book of
Romans when Paul refers to him as my "fellow worker" and not
just as a true son: "Timothy, my fellow worker, sends you his
greetings, as do Lucius, Jason, and Sosipater, my fellow Jews"
(Romans 16:21 NLT).

Timothy had developed beyond being a son or apprentice
to being a fellow worker in the ministry. That's why Paul never
hesitated to send him to Ephesus to lead the church. Even
though Timothy was young, Paul set a platform for him to excel
and thrive as the bishop of Ephesus.

Unlock their shine. Catholic priest James Keller had a
powerful leadership proverb that says, "A candle loses nothing by
lighting another candle."[2] Legacy-minded leaders are intentional
about bringing out the best in their followers. They go out of their
way to unleash the potential and the shine of those around them
without feeling insecure or intimidated by their progress.

If you cannot afford opportunities to those you lead—so
they shine and blossom—you will end up being the only giant

surrounded by an ocean of dwarfs. That means that all that will be left of your legacy will be an ocean of leadership dwarfs who never grew to their full potential because you withheld yourself from helping them unleash their best.

> *"If you want one year of prosperity, grow grain. If you want ten years of prosperity, grow trees. But if you want a hundred years of prosperity, grow people."—Chinese Proverb*

Displayer Leaders Model a "Posterity Mentality"

Having a posterity mentality is simply doing things that will outlive you and will continue to impact others long after you have exited the leadership landscape. This is achieved not only by how many people you have developed but also by how you have displayed those people by providing platforms of exposure.

Leading with posterity in mind is not just something that should happen at the end of our leadership journey. To live with posterity is to be aware of the small positive things you do on a daily basis, which add value to those you lead and to your organization. The small and big decisions you make each and every day add up to your long-term influence. Leaders understand that every little positive step they take each day has a ripple effect into the future.

> "Leaders with a posterity mentality do things that will outlive them and continue impacting others long after they have exited the leadership landscape."

Renowned environmentalist and founder of the Green Belt Movement, the late Wangari Maathai modeled a great example of leading with posterity in mind.

In 2004, she became the first African woman to receive the Nobel Peace Prize. She understood that every small contribution to preserve the environment—especially the forest cover in Kenya and Africa—would go a long way in helping future generations have a clean environment, predictable weather patterns, and an atmosphere conducive to life and growth.

When she was awarded the Nobel Peace Prize, Maathai shared the story that inspired her tireless efforts to conserve forests in Africa, despite the fact her life was threatened because of her work:

> The story of the hummingbird is about this huge forest being consumed by a fire. All the animals in the forest come out and they are transfixed as they watch the forest burning and they feel very overwhelmed, very powerless, except this little hummingbird. It says, "I'm going to do something about the fire!"
>
> So it flies to the nearest stream and takes a drop of water. It puts it on the fire, and goes up and down, up and down in

repetitive circles as fast as it can. In the meantime, all the other animals, much bigger animals like the elephant with a big trunk that could bring much more water, are standing there helpless.

They say to the hummingbird, "What do you think you can do? You are too little. This fire is too big. Your wings are too little and your beak is so small that you can only bring a small drop of water at a time."

But as they continue to discourage it, it turns to them without wasting any time and tells them, "I am doing the best I can."[3]

Maathai went on to say that we should all be like a hummingbird. For her, she didn't want to be like the animals, watching the planet going down the drain. Instead she chose to be a hummingbird, doing the best she could.

Displayer Leaders are Courageous

Jehoiada is one of the least discussed leaders in the Old Testament. But this priest was a discreet displayer leader who courageously developed and set the stage for one of the youngest, if not *the* youngest, kings in Israel.

Jehoiada almost risked his own life to set the stage for the young King Joash, earning Jehoiada a spot in the annals of displayer leaders in Scripture. His story is recorded in the books of 2 Kings 11 and 2 Chronicles 22:

When Athaliah the mother of Ahaziah saw that her son was dead, she proceeded to destroy the whole royal family. But

Jehosheba, the daughter of King Jehoram and sister of Ahaziah, took Joash son of Ahaziah and stole him away from among the royal princes, who were about to be murdered. She put him and his nurse in a bedroom to hide him from Athaliah; so he was not killed. He remained hidden with his nurse at the temple of the LORD for six years while Athaliah ruled the land.

In the seventh year Jehoiada sent for the commanders of units of a hundred, the Carites and the guards and had them brought to him at the temple of the LORD. He made a covenant with them and put them under oath at the temple of the LORD. Then he showed them the king's son. ...

Jehoiada brought out the king's son and put the crown on him; he presented him with a copy of the covenant and proclaimed him king. They anointed him, and the people clapped their hands and shouted, "Long live the king!"

2 Kings 11:1–4, 12

Queen Athaliah usurped the throne after the death of her son and then killed all her grandchildren except Joash, who was hidden by the wife of the priest Jehoiada (Joahs's aunt) in the priest's house. After six years, the priest orchestrated events that facilitated Joash's return to the throne by staging a coup that dethroned Athaliah.

This priest risked his life to preserve, tutor, and prepare the true heir to the throne of David—the little boy who came to him as a baby, grew up under his wing, and blossomed into a good man. Joash was successful because he had the nurturing of a good mentor: Jehoiada, the priest.

Displayer leaders must exhibit great courage and ride against the waves of conventional leadership thinking, which says if you set the stage for others you become irrelevant.

We learn important leadership lessons from the priest Jehoiada, lessons which are essential for any leader who aspires to be an effective displayer.

He mentored Joash. Displayer leaders understand the importance of taking upcoming leaders under them as apprentices; they realize that the ultimate responsibility of every great leader is to make other leaders.

He affirmed Joash as king. Displayer leaders know how to spot potential and call it out of people. A simple act of affirming those you are developing goes a long way in building their confidence, enabling them to thrive despite their age, doubts, and inadequacies.

He held Joash accountable. Jehoiada led the young king in making a covenant with God and the people of Israel to remain faithful and serve the people according to the law of God. He constantly reinforced godly leadership and priorities over the king's life for as long as he lived.

Like Jehoiada, leaders must be courageous enough to take calculated risks. Legacy mindedness requires courage. Courage to go against the grain of conventional leadership. Courage to overcome the fear of thinking you become irrelevant when you create a platform for others.

As this book concludes, I want to highlight one significant question every great leader-maker should ask themselves: "What will be my legacy?"

We should never count ourselves successful until we have developed a team that guarantees the future success of our organizations and the continuity of the vision God has given us.

I pray that this book has sparked a burning desire and birthed a burden inside you to urgently start thinking about creating a legacy that will go beyond you and extend into future generations—to become those who seed out what God has placed in you.

I am convinced that this is possible if you intentionally identify a team that you serve, envision, empower, and display, so that they are able to execute their learnings for kingdom impact.

May your leadership journey bear fruits that will outlive you and leave an indelible mark in people's hearts and transform society for the glory of God.

SEED IT OUT REFLECTIONS

1. What are some of the ways you can leverage your influence and credibility to endorse upcoming leaders?

2. What are some of the virtues and values you want to inculcate in your life that you have seen in leaders who have impacted the world in powerful ways?

3. What practical things will you do as a leader to model and inspire legacy conscious leadership?

4. How could you use your influence to create opportunities for others?

5. What platforms do you have as a leader that you could share with others to help them grow?

6. What can you do to inspire people to better hone their skills and become legendary leaders in their own right?

7. What opportunities do the people you are developing need to expand their influence and sharpen their competence?

8. What are some of the practical things you can do to discover more possibilities for fulfilling the potential of those you are leading?

9. How can you hold those you are leading accountable to help them develop strong integrity and firm discipline to excel in leadership?

Acknowledgments

The thoughts in this book are a result of many years of learning, working under a great leader, and being part of numerous teams.

Different people have influenced my philosophy of leadership. Of notable mention is Bishop J. B. Masinde, the founder and senior pastor of Deliverance Church Umoja, whom I have had the privilege of serving under and whom has significantly shaped my leadership.

I would like to thank the pastoral staff and the serve team at Deliverance Church Umoja whom I serve alongside. Much of my leadership learning has taken place in this context.

Thanks to the M28 Leaders Network, a discipleship and leadership development network of pastors. Interfacing with these great leaders has helped me strive to be better every day.

I want to sincerely thank Boniface Nyoike, who patiently sat with me and helped bring out the thoughts in this book; not forgetting Edith Chebet who read through the earlier manuscript.

I would also like to thank the team at 100 Movements Publishing and especially Anna Robinson, for her expertise in editing and guidance of the process. Your contribution has sharpened the content and given it clarity. Thank you for your attention to detail.

Finally, I would like to thank my wife, Jeniffer Amisi, and our daughter, Kristi Amisi, who have both cheered me on as I put together this book.

This book is what it is because of you all.

Notes

FOREWORD: BISHOP JOHN B. MASINDE

1   John C. Maxwell, *The 360 Degree Leader: Developing Your Influence from Anywhere in the Organization* (New York: HarperCollins Leadership, 2011).

INTRODUCTION

1   John Stanko, *So Many Leaders…So Little Leadership* (Mobile, Alabama: Evergreen Press, 2000), 5–158.

2   https://movementleaderscollective.com.

1 REALITY CHECK

1   John C. Maxwell, *The 5 Levels of Leadership: Proven Steps to Maximize Your Potential* (Nashville, Tennessee: Center Street, 2011), 5–289.

2   Twah JALi, https://www.facebook.com/twahjali.

3   Jithamini International, https://www.facebook.com/jithamini.international.

2 SERVE

1   Robert Greenleaf, *Servant Leadership: A Journey into the Nature of Legitimate Power and Greatness [25th Anniversary Edition]* (New York: Paulist Press, 2002), 16–21.

2   Harpeth Hall, "Everybody Can Be Great, Because Everybody Can Serve," *Harpeth Hall*, January 15, 2021, https://www.harpethhall.org/news/p/~board/n/post/ everybody-can-be-great-because-everybody-can-serve.

3   See, for example, Jack Kelly, "The Way Companies Treat Their Employees Will Determine if They'll Be Winners or Losers in the War for Talent," *Forbes*, June 20, 2021, https:// www.forbes.com/sites/jackkelly/2021/06/20/the-way- companies-treat-their-employees-will-determine-if-theyll- be-winners-or-losers-in-the-war-for-talent/.

4   Craig Groeschel (@craiggroeschel), Twitter post, April 12, 2018, https://twitter.com/craiggroeschel/status/ 984491223976169480.

5   Adapted from "10 Of The Most Inspiring Leaders Of All Time: Remarkable Stories Of Iconic Trail Blazers Who Went From Adversity To Extraordinary & Redefined Leadership," *Inspiring Leadership Now*, April 2, 2020, https://www.inspiringleadershipnow.com/most-inspiring- leaders-redefine-leadership/.

6   Patrick Lencioni, *The Motive: Why So Many Leaders Abdicate Their Most Important Responsibilities* (New York: Jossey-Bass, 2020), 22–192.

7   "Supreme Commander of the Allied Forces – Dwight D.

Eisenhower," *Business and Leadership*, May 3, 2019, https://www.businessandleadership.com/leadership/item/dwight-d-eisenhower-allied-forces-supreme-commander/.

8   Michael Shinagel, "The Paradox of Leadership," *Harvard Division of Continuing Education*, July 3, 2013, https://professional.dce.harvard.edu/blog/the-paradox-of-leadership/.

9   Mike Breen, *Covenant and Kingdom: The DNA of the Bible* (Pawleys Island: 3DM, 2010), 141–144.

10 Maxwell, *The 360° Degree Leader*, 285–290.

11 https://www.thefreedictionary.com/purpose.

12 Slingshot Group (@slingshotgroup), Twitter post, November 10, 2019, https://twitter.com/slingshotgroup/status/1193623632918040576.

13 Patrick Lencioni, *The Ideal Team Player: How to Recognize and Cultivate the Three Essential Virtues* (San Francisco: Jossey-Bass, 2016).

14 T. D. Jakes, "T. D. Jakes Quotes," *AZ Quotes*, https://www.azquotes.com/quote/522194.

3   ENVISION

1   See Luke 6:39.

2   *The Boy Who Harnessed the Wind*, directed by Chiewetel Ejiofor (UK: Netflix, 2019), streaming.

3   "These Are the 30 People Under 30 Changing the World," *Time*, December 6, 2013, https://ideas.time.com/2013/12/06/these-are-the-30-people-under-30-changing-the-world/slide/all/.

4   "Rosa Parks and the Montgomery Bus Boycott," *U.S. History*, https://www.ushistory.org/us/54b.asp.

5   John Blake, "The one thing about Martin Luther King Jr.'s greatness everyone keeps missing," *CNN*, January 20, 2020, https://edition.cnn.com/2020/01/20/us/martin-luther-king-jr-listener-blake/index.html.

6   Alan Redpath, *Victorious Christian Service: Studies in the Book of Nehemiah* (Scotts Valley, CA: CreateSpace Independent Publishing Platform, 2013), 15–26.

7   Charles R. Swindoll, *Hand Me Another Brick: How Effective Leaders Motivate Themselves and Others* (Nashville: Thomas Nelson, 2006), 40–62.

8   Marcus Buckingham, *The One Thing You Need to Know: ... About Great Managing, Great Leading, and Sustained Individual Success* (New York: Free Press, 2005), 1–15.

9   Roy Johnson and John Eaton, *Influencing People* (New York, NY: DK Publishing Inc, 2002), 6–10.

10 "Warren Buffet: Three Things I Look For in a Person," *Farnam Street*, https://fs.blog/warren-buffett-the-three-things-i-look-for-in-a-person.

11 Rick Warren, *The Purpose Driven Life: What on Earth Am I Here For?* (Grand Rapids: Zondervan, 2013), quoted in "Quotable Quotes," *GoodReads,* https://www.goodreads.com/quotes/383930-humility-is-not-thinking-less-of-yourself-it-is-thinking.

4 EMPOWER

1   Myles Munroe, *The Spirit of Leadership: Cultivating the Attributes That Influence Human Action* (Kensington, PA: Whitaker House, 2005), 223–271.

2   "5 Leadership lessons from African leader Robert Collymore," *Stellenbosch Business School*, May 2, 2019, https://usb-ed.com/5-leadership-lessons-from-african-leader-robert-collymore/.

3   Ibid.

4   "Famous quotes by Howard Hendricks," *Quotes*, https://www.quotes.net/authors/Howard+Hendricks.

5   Dr. Jasmine Renner, *365 Daily Wisdom and Creativity: Confessions and Affirmations* (CreateSpace Independent Publishing Platform, 2012), https://www.ebookit.com/tools/pd/Bo/eBookIt/booktitle-365-Daily-Wisdom-and-Creativity—Confessions-and-Affirmations#null.

6   Dan Reiland, *Amplified Leadership: 5 Practices to Establish Influence, Build People, and Impact Others for a Lifetime* (Lake Mary, FL: Charisma House, 2011), 11.

7   Mike Breen, *Multiplying Missional Leaders: From Half-Hearted Volunteers to a Mobilized Kingdom Force* (3D Ministries Publishing, 2012).

8   Ibid., 59–61.

9   Michael McKinney, "Ronald Reagan on Leadership," *Leadership Now*, February 6, 2011, https://www.

leadershipnow.com/leadingblog/2011/02/ronald_
reagan_on_leadership.html.

5 DISPLAY

1   Pete's name and the company names have been changed to
protect anonymity.

2   https://www.goodreads.com/quotes/220820-a-candle-
loses-nothing-by-lighting-another-candle.

3   "Wangari Maathai – 'I will be a hummingbird,'" *The Kids
Should See This,* https://thekidshouldseethis.com/post/
wangari-maathai-i-will-be-a-hummingbird.

About the Author

Oscar Amisi is the senior associate pastor of Deliverance Church Umoja and the lead trainer at SeeditOut, an initiative that aims to build and equip high-impact servant leaders in the marketplace. In this latter role, he has trained and consulted widely with different organizations.

Oscar is a member of the Institute of Directors Kenya and serves as one of the council members of Movement Leaders Collective, a global community for movement leaders and a catalyst for movement leadership. He was also recently invited to be part of the ARC (Association of Related Churches) East African hub pioneering team.

www.m28network.org

www.movementleaderscollective.com

www.arcchurches.com

www.seeditout.org